THE WAY THEY PLAY

THE HARD ROCK MASTERS

by HP Newquist and Rich Maloof

Backbeat Books
San Francisco

Published by Backbeat Books
600 Harrison Street, San Francisco, CA 94107
www.backbeatbooks.com
email: books@musicplayer.com

An imprint of CMP Information
Publishers of *Guitar Player*, *Bass Player*, *Keyboard*, and *EQ* magazines

CMP
United Business Media

Distributed to the book trade in the US and Canada by
Publishers Group West, 1700 Fourth Street, Berkeley, CA 94710

Distributed to the music trade in the US and Canada by
Hal Leonard Publishing, P.O. Box 13819, Milwaukee, WI 53213

Cover and text design: Richard Leeds — bigwigdesign.com
Cover photo: Rahav Segev/Photopass.com
Composition by Michael Cutter

Library of Congress Cataloging-in-Publication Data

Newquist, H. P. (Harvey P.)
The hard rock masters / by HP Newquist and Rich Maloof.
    p. cm. — (The way they play)
ISBN 0-87930-813-3 (alk. paper)
1. Guitar—Instruction and study. 2. Rock music—Instruction and study.
3. Guitarists—Biography. I. Maloof, Rich. II. Title. III. Series.

MT580.N485 2004
787.87'166'0922—dc22
                          2004019901

Printed in the United States of America
04 05 06 07 08   5 4 3 2 1

CONTENTS

INTRODUCTION

More than any other style of music, hard rock is defined by its guitars. After all, you can rock 'n' roll with synths and organs, but you can't be serious about going at it *really* hard without a solidbody guitar cranked to 10.

Hard rock is not to be confused with metal. First off, hard rock invites a few more styles into its bedroom—notably some of the more experimental styles of the '60s and '70s. As the genre's best players have revealed, hard rock guitar is heavily dosed by the blues, punk, pop, rockabilly, and even folk. Metal, on the other hand, exists primarily to crush your skull with minor-chorded dirges and riffs constructed from pig iron and prestressed concrete.

Hard rock also allows for more stylistic flexibility than metal. This is not to say it's any better or worse than metal, just different. For instance, it's hard to infuse metal with psychedelia or pop melodies. Yet you can pull it off—if you're really good—as a hard rock guitarist. Look no further than the early Van Halen or Foo Fighters albums. You can use that music as the soundtrack to smash stuff up, and you can still sing along with it. It's party music, particularly good for dangerous parties.

One uniting characteristic of the players we've covered is that they know how to make a mountain of music out of a molehill of material. Ninety percent of what you hear in their solos comes directly out of the pentatonic and blues scales. Effects seldom stray from manually controlled devices like wah pedals and whammy bars. And the songs, a few exceptions aside, tend to be three- and four-chord wonders (or even less) that sit neatly within one key. Take two guys at opposite ends of the spectrum, like Eddie Van Halen and Angus Young. Eddie swirls hundreds of sounds into a solo break, while Angus is a notorious note miser. But, pound for pound, there are more chord changes in AC/DC tunes than in Van Halen songs.

Even though simplicity and straightforwardness characterize the vast majority of our players, there's not a single one of them that sounds like any other. Angus Young, Ace Frehley, Eddie Van Halen, and Dave Grohl may each have reveled in two- and three-chord rock, but you can tell the difference between them from the first beat of the first bar. The same goes for Jerry Cantrell, Dave Navarro, and Dean DeLeo, each of whom owes a significant hard rock debt to heavy metal, and whose best songs can be reduced to compelling and simple riffs and chord progressions.

These players represent the finest of two generations of hard rock guitarists. Remarkably, all are playing by and large within the confines of a style defined almost 40 years ago. It's how these players put it all together—how they take the familiar or the simple and twist it into something new and interesting—that makes them hard rock masters. Most of them have found a unique way to mix their own musical tastes with their predecessors', whether those predecessors are Tony Iommi, Jimi Hendrix, and Jimmy Page, or, just as often, Angus Young and Ace Frehley. In guitar playing, what goes around comes around.

It's one thing to read about these players, and another to hear the essence of their playing. But to get a real feel for what these guitarists have done, you have to go back and listen to their albums. Really *listen*, which can be especially hard when you are intimately familiar with a recording. Better yet, listen with a guitar in your hands and the idea in your head that it is all doable. Van Halen probably inspired as many people to pick up the guitar as he did people to quit. Decide which camp you're in. If you still want to play, take a favorite passage of his and plant yourself in front of the speakers until you can do it without a hitch. One of our goals with this book is to get you over that hump, to show you that the playing styles of these guitarists are really approachable. Despite what we hear, these guys are musicians, not magicians.

In revisiting all the albums produced by these guitarists and their bands, we were amazed at just how innovative these guys were, and one of our criteria for including players was whether their music has stood the test of time. Some—like Dave Grohl and Dave Navarro—sound fresh because they're relatively new, while recordings by Kim Thayil and Eddie Van Halen remain more more listenable and groundbreaking than the majority of crap that passes for modern music. So get some of the recommended cuts, listen to them on a pair of good speakers, and be prepared to get shellacked by 6-string land mines. Then get ready to detonate a few of your own.

—HP Newquist and Rich Maloof

NOTATIONAL SYMBOLS

The following symbols are used in *The Hard Rock Masters* to notate fingerings, techniques, and effects commonly used in guitar music. Certain symbols are found in either the tablature or the standard notation only, not both. For clarity, consult both systems.

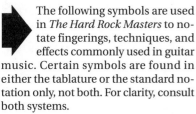 : Left-hand fingering is designated by small Arabic numerals near note heads (1=first finger, 2=middle finger, 3=third finger, 4=little finger, t=thumb).

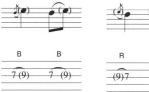 : Right-hand fingering designated by letters (p=thumb, i=first finger, m=middle finger, a=third finger, c=little finger).

 : A circled number (1-6) indicates the string on which a note is to be played.

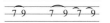 : Pick downstroke.

V : Pick upstroke.

Bend: Play the first note and bend to the pitch of the equivalent fret position shown in parentheses.

Reverse Bend: Pre-bend the note to the specified pitch/fret position shown in parentheses. Play, then release to indicated pitch/fret.

Hammer-on: From lower to higher note(s). Individual notes may also be hammered.

Pull-off: From higher to lower note(s).

Slide: Play first note and slide up or down to the next pitch. If the notes are tied, pick only the first. If no tie is present, pick both.

A slide symbol before or after a single note indicates a slide to or from an undetermined pitch.

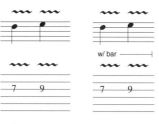

Finger vibrato. **Bar vibrato.**

Bar dips, dives, and bends: Numerals and fractions indicate distance of bar bends in half-steps.

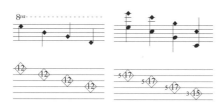

Natural harmonics. **Artificial harmonics.**

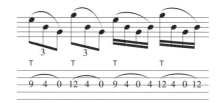

Pick-hand tapping: Notes are hammered with a pick-hand finger, usually followed by additional hammer-ons and pull-offs.

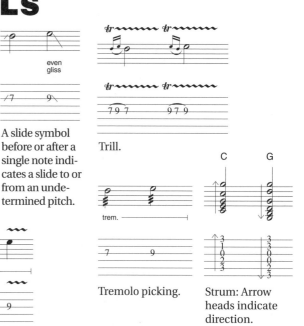

Trill.

Tremolo picking. **Strum:** Arrow heads indicate direction.

HOW TABLATURE WORKS

The horizontal lines represent the guitar's strings, the top line standing for the high *E*. The numbers designate the frets to be played. For instance, a 2 positioned on the first line would mean play the 2nd fret on the first string (0 indicates an open string). Time values are indicated on the standard notation staff seen directly above the tablature. Special symbols and instructions appear between the standard and tablature staves.

CHORD DIAGRAMS

In all chord diagrams, vertical lines represent the strings, and horizontal lines represent the frets. The following symbols are used:

▬▬▬ Nut; indicates first position.

X Muted string, or string not played.

○ Open string.

⌒ Barre (partial or full).

● Placement of left-hand fingers.

||| Roman numerals indicate the fret at which a chord is located.

Arabic numerals indicate left-hand fingering.

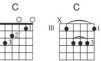

CHAPTER 1
Ace Frehley of Kiss

Ace Frehley may be most unusual guitar hero in the history of hard rock. Early indications were that he and his band mates in Kiss were destined only for novelty status and less than 15 minutes of fame. Yet Ace's inherently cool and controlled approach to guitar playing struck a nerve in the mid-'70s. He played hard rock without having to beat the life out of the guitar, and still created a huge sound that rocked the foundation of every stadium you can think of.

While creating hard rock by building on the blues-rock foundation of '60s guitar icons, Frehley's lead playing would hardly be considered in the same league as Eric Clapton's or Keith Richards's. His playing was rarely frenetic, and he stuck to the safety of the blues box in his solos while relying heavily on bending single notes over and over. Yet, attired in his boots and space costume, and with Les Paul in hand, Ace created an entirely new look and sound for lead guitarists. It wasn't evident at the time, but Ace Frehley would go on to inspire as many people to pick up the guitar as did the British Invasion guitarists who inspired him.

BIOGRAPHY

Paul Daniel Frehley (that's pronounced *FRAY-lee*, kids) was born on April 27, 1950, in the Bronx, New York. Everyone in his family, including his parents, played musical instruments. His older brother was a guitarist who played a lot of folk music, including songs by Paul Simon and Peter, Paul & Mary. An admittedly rebellious youth, young Paul wasn't interested in much of this until he heard his first amplified guitar. Then he took a serious interest. His brother taught him the basics, and his father bought him an electric guitar for his 14th birthday. The British invasion and Hendrix were big influences on Paul, who dedicated himself to his twin pursuits of guitar playing and drawing.

Paul and his brother played in several bands together around New York in the late '60s, performing covers of tunes by British rock bands. That changed in 1973 when Paul answered a music ad in New York's *Village Voice* newspaper seeking a lead guitarist. The band was Wicked Lester, led by bass player (and former grade-school teacher) Gene Simmons and guitarist Paul Stanley. Simmons and Stanley had plans to make Wicked Lester a big-time glam band, and Paul Frehley, with his spacey attitude, mismatched clothes, and knowledge of hard rock guitar styles, fit the bill perfectly. The only thing he had to do was change his first name, since Paul Stanley already laid claim to that. Frehley adopted a nickname from school—he was evidently an "ace" at getting his friends dates—and the band, with Peter Criss on drums, was born. Only now it was to be called *Kiss*.

With its clown paint and kabuki makeup, Kiss had a difficult time getting taken seriously. Their riffs were Zeppelin, Stones, and Cream knockoffs, and they stuck closely to a four-chord verse/chorus format. Strictly from a guitar perspective, their first three studio albums were less than stellar affairs. But live, Kiss had the excitement of a punk circus—and they were actually more skilled than punk musicians and circus clowns. Thus it took a live album—a double live album at that—to capture the enormity and explosiveness of the band's sound. *Alive!* introduced Kiss to the world, and suddenly the band wasn't quite so easy to dismiss. It was picked up by seemingly every teenage boy in the country, many of whom decided that they, too, wanted to be as cool as Ace Frehley and his smoking Les Paul.

With the breakthrough of 1975's *Alive!*, Kiss was faced with the task of coming up with a proper studio album for its legions of new fans. Employing producer Bob Ezrin of Alice Cooper fame, the band recorded *Destroyer*, an album that was equal parts thundering rock, well-orchestrated and well-crafted tunes, and studio wizardry. From the opening riff and sonic cannon blast of "Detroit Rock City" to sledgehammer tracks like "God of Thunder" and "Do You Love Me," the album perfectly captured the larger-than-life imagery and sound of Kiss. *Destroyer* was the right album at the right time in their career, and Kiss became a certifiable hard rock phenomenon.

The band followed with two noteworthy albums, *Rock and Roll Over* (featuring "Calling Dr. Love" and "I Want You") and *Love Gun* (with the Ritchie Blackmore-esque "I Stole Your Love" and the psychedelic solo to "Almost Human") before each member released his own solo record in 1978. A promotional stunt that backfired, none of the albums sold well (the joke was that they shipped gold and were returned platinum). Nonetheless, Frehley broke into the Top 20 with his single "New York Groove" and proved that he was more than capable of holding his own against Simmons and Stanley in the writing and playing department.

Simmons and Stanley kicked Ace out of the band in 1982. The rationale at the time was that Kiss needed new blood and enthusiasm after producing lame albums such as *Music from the Elder* and *Creatures of the Night*. In reality, Frehley was having serious substance abuse problems coupled with a penchant for wrecking expensive cars. He was replaced by Vinnie Vincent, a Frehley look-alike with major attitude issues who lasted barely two years before getting the boot. Mark St. John was hired as Vincent's replacement in 1984 for *Animalize*, but a diagnosis of Reiter's syndrome (an arthritic condition) prevented him from playing with the band. Finally, session guitarist Bruce Kulick came in and established himself as the band's "new" lead guitarist for the next decade. In a small-world coincidence, when Ace had auditioned for Wicked Lester, he had followed the guitarist who was

CHECKLIST ✓

Guitars . . . . Gibson Les Pauls

Setup . . . . Standard

Strings . . . . Gibson Ace Frehley
Signature, .009–.046

Pickups . . . . DiMarzio Super Distortions,
set to treble pickup

Amplification . . . Marshall JCM900,
Peavey 5150 II head,
Marshall 4x12 cabinets

Effects . . . . None worth mentioning

Tone . . . . Biting, sharp, with a high
treble quotient

Attack . . . . Not as heavy as it sounds;
tends to be restrained like the
British masters, not violent

**Signature
traits** . . . . Sustained power chords,
repeated bent notes,
wide vibrato

Influences . . . . . Jimi Hendrix, Eric Clapton,
Jimmy Page

**Overall
approach** . . . . Cool and controlled, but big
enough to fill any arena

SELECTED DISCOGRAPHY

With Kiss:
Kiss (Casablanca/Mercury, 1974)
Hotter Than Hell (Casablanca/ Mercury, 1974)
Dressed to Kill (Casablanca/ Mercury, 1975)
Alive! (Casablanca/Mercury, 1975)
Destroyer (Casablanca/Mercury, 1975)
Rock and Roll Over (Casablanca/ Mercury, 1976)
Love Gun (Casablanca/Mercury, 1977)
Alive II (Casablanca/Mercury, 1977)

Solo albums:
Ace Frehley (Casablanca, 1978)
Frehley's Comet (Megaforce, 1987)
Trouble Walkin' (Megaforce, 1989)

RECOMMENDED CUTS
"100,000 Years" (*Alive!*)
"Cold Gin" (*Alive!*)
"Deuce" (*Alive!*)
"She" (*Alive!*)
"Love Gun" (*Love Gun*)
"Detroit Rock City" (*Destroyer*)
"New York Groove" (*Ace Frehley*)
"Shock Me" (*Love Gun*)
"Hotter Than Hell" (*Alive!*)
"Got to Choose" (*Alive!*)
"Firehouse" (*Alive!*)
"Almost Human" (*Love Gun*)

the leading contender for the job: Bob Kulick, Bruce's older brother.

While Kiss produced some passable records during this period (from 1983's *Lick It Up* to '92's *Revenge*) and some truly horrific ones, Frehley pursued a solo career that existed under the radar of everyone but diehard fans. He recorded several solo albums with an on-again off-again group called Frehley's Comet. The records suffered from substandard material, and Frehley's playing lacked the spark it once had with Kiss.

During the early 1990s, even though he was laboring in relative obscurity (the specter of Kiss loomed large, and Simmons and Stanley kept the spotlight on themselves), Ace's name started appearing in interviews with hard rock guitarists. While it had once been popular to dismiss Frehley's brand of big and simple power-chord rock, it seemed that now everyone was eager to claim Frehley as their earliest inspiration and influence. A whole generation came out the closet to acknowledge Ace's showmanship and biting riffs, including Jerry Cantrell of Alice in Chains, Dimebag Darrell of Pantera, Kim Thayil of Soundgarden, Mike McCready of Pearl Jam, Dean DeLeo of Stone Temple Pilots, and Scott Ian of Anthrax.

This sudden outpouring of early- and mid-'90s adoration may or may not have had a bearing on the band's decision to bring Ace back into the fold during Kiss's 1996 appearance on *MTV Unplugged*. The obvious fan affection for Frehley (and returning drummer Criss) showed Simmons and Stanley that there was a huge audience waiting to relive the early Kiss years. Frehley signed back on with the band, although not as a full partner, because Simmons and Stanley were legally the only real members of the team; anyone else who came through the door was treated as a hired gun, complete with contracts and salaries. The original Kiss toured the world, reigniting audience fervor that was as intense as it had been during their *Destroyer* heyday.

However, the resulting studio record, *Psycho Circus*, was mediocre at the very best (with the exception of the title cut), and fans gave it the same lack of love they gave *The Elder* and its ilk. Dissension reappeared in the band, and Frehley was fired yet again. He has been replaced in the band's current incarnation by Black 'n Blue's Tommy Thayer—the first stand-in to wear Ace's distinctive makeup. Not cool.

It's doubtful that we'll hear much from Ace again, and, unfortunately, we'll probably never see anyone quite like him again. But as a guitarist, he mastered the simplicity of hard rock, creating a signature sound with simple basics—equipment, chords, and solos—that has had a lasting effect on how to use the guitar to deliver the maximum dose of rock 'n' roll.

GEAR & SETUP

Ace has always—with rare exceptions—used Gibson Les Paul Deluxes, Customs, and Standards. (The slogan that appeared on the early Kiss albums—"Kiss uses Gibson guitars because they want the best"—pretty much sums up his thinking.) After the first album, which featured a tobacco sunburst Deluxe, he started using a three-pickup '74 cherry sunburst Les Paul. His solo records were usually cut with a '59 Standard. Frehley's older Les Pauls retain their original PAF pickups, although he puts DiMarzio Super Distortion pickups in newer models.

In the studio Ace has used both Fender Stratocasters and Telecasters to double the rhythm parts he plays on his Les Pauls. Those guitars are never used for solos. In live shows he has used other instruments, including Flying V's, Explorers, and a few doublenecks. It should be noted that during his solo period he also used Washburn guitars, with the Washburn Wonder Bar tremolo system (which he claims, in retrospect, he didn't like).

In 1997 Gibson introduced an Ace Frehley signature Les Paul to capitalize on Frehley's renewed popularity and Kiss's return to touring with the original members. At the time, the deal specified that it would be the only three-pickup sunburst model produced by Gibson.

Frehley was once one of the most aggressive collectors around, having snatched up literally hundreds of guitars during his glory days with Kiss. Those guitars were sold when times got tight post-Kiss, and the ones that survived were his Les Pauls.

Though not known for his acoustic playing, Ace does own several Guilds, Yamahas, and Martins. His only real step outside of the world of standard solidbodies was when he used an Avatar guitar synth on his '78 solo record.

For his strings, Ace commonly uses .009–.046 sets. His action is quite high, usually from ⅛" to ⅜" off the fretboard. Gibson, which saw no end to Ace's enduring popularity, even introduced signature strings in the mid 1990s. He uses Herco Flex 75 picks.

Marshalls have been Frehley's amp of choice, and he updated them at various stages of his career. His main amp was a JCM900 going through Marshall 4x12 cabinets. By the time he rejoined Kiss, he was using the Marshall 2100 SL-X Super Lead-eXtended Master Volume 100-watt amp along with a Peavey 5150 II head. His cabinets were custom-finished Marshall 1960BV 4x12s with Celestion Vintage 30 speakers. In a display of characteristic overstatement, Kiss has gone onstage with as many as 44 custom mirror-fronted Marshall heads and cabs.

Although known for his Marshalls, Frehley has also been a fan of Laney amps. He claims they're more versatile than the Marshalls, although they require a little more work to get a biting lead-guitar sound. He played Laneys extensively during his solo years before switching back to Marshalls.

Ace prefers to play with a straight sound and a rich natural tone in the studio, which means no effects and no reverb—most of the effects on the Kiss albums were added in the mix. He almost always uses the lead pickup and keeps the rhythm pickup off, as evidenced with the occasional stuttering effect he would get by rapidly switching the pickup selector between positions. Onstage he used effects sparingly, for instance to highlight solo passages or some specific aspect of the show. These have included a digital delay for the smoking guitar solo, a Zoom pedal, and a Mu-Tron Octave Divider.

Kiss is as much about appearance as about rock 'n' roll, so it's only appropriate to add some cosmetic guitar information here. Apparently Ace liked the look of the three-pickup guitar so much that some of the two-pickup guitars he used live were outfitted with a plastic rectangle to give the appearance of three pickups, because he didn't want to actually modify them with additional pickups.

As for all those modified guitars that he used onstage: one was a "rocket launcher" that shot fireworks from a cylinder that ran behind the neck and on the headstock. The device was triggered by his thumb on the guitar body. The infamous smoking guitar started when he shoved a smoke bomb in the potentiometer cavity on the guitar's backside, and the smoke seeped out through the cable holes and pickup casing (the wick hung out the back and was lit by a cigarette lighter). It got more complex when he added a halogen bulb in place of the rarely-used rhythm pickup, and then created a switch to turn on the light while the smoke poured out, giving it that electric glow. Originally, the light was powered by an electric cable that ran up next to his guitar cord (and was activated by his roadie). Later on these were battery-controlled devices.

STYLE & TECHNIQUE

Ace's power-chord rock, along with his simple riffs—little speed or shredding here—helped define his playing. He likes to plug in, keep the effects to a minimum, and go for the tone. Like the best and most recognizable hard rockers, Frehley bases his sound on pushing the relationship between a Les Paul through a Marshall stack to its decibel limits. There isn't anything else in his signal chain to mess up the sound, which helps produce his raw and razor-like signature tone.

Almost all of Ace's playing influences come from the British invasion era, notably Jimmy Page and Eric Clapton. Frehley's power chords were pure Zeppelin and Cream, while the partial chords and suspensions he favored (as in the opening of the Kiss hit "Rock and Roll All Nite") are right out of the Keith Richards book. His solos had the bluesy simplicity of Page's early work, while his emphasis on pure, unaffected tone has more in common with Clapton, as did his use of a slow, wide vibrato that seemed consistent with his forever sleepy-looking eyes. In keeping with his mien, he had a restrained approach to playing that was completely different from the volatile styles of his contemporaries.

His soloing is, by any standard, traditional, even a bit primitive. His signature lick, a series of bent and repeated notes in the pentatonic box, became so closely identified with Ace that anyone else who attempted to play it would be accused of copping directly from him. This, even though he copped it from Page.

Ace rarely plans solos, preferring to wing it in the studio by working around some core ideas or licks—a habit that he says arose from the fact that Gene and Paul never liked the solos he prepared in advance.

LESSON

In **Ex. 1**, Ace harvests the history of classic rock guitar. Pieces of Chuck Berry and even Jimi Hendrix—both via Keith Richards—are evident in the hammered chords. Kiss loved to use the technique in their two-guitar arrangements, often with one guitar riding them out and another planting big chords underneath or big leads on top.

Your first hammer-on is at the 12th fret. It implies a suspended sound, though you're really hammering from *G* to *C*. A similar move follows at the 5th fret (*C* to *F*); then it's Hendrix hammers, all of them on double-stops, before returning to the top of the pattern.

Ex. 1

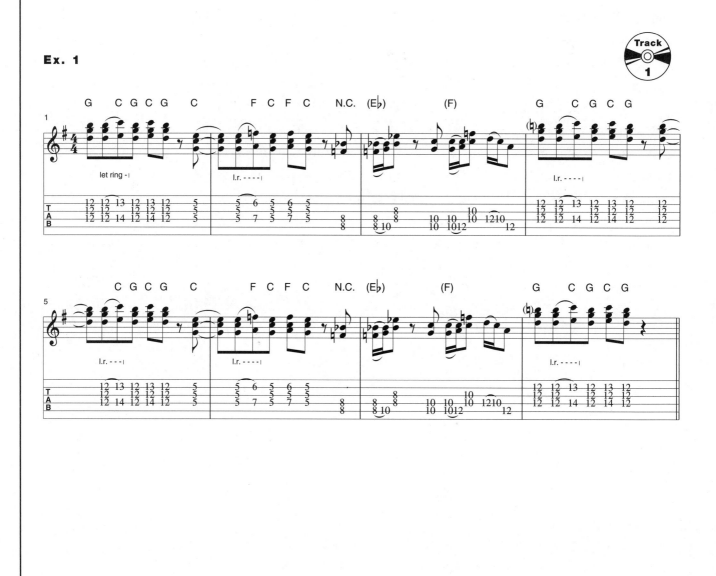

Even when limited to pentatonics, Ace could lay down a melodic lead for intros and breaks. The phrases that make up **Ex. 2** come in neat two-bar packets, in most cases with a whole-note held for the second bar. Note the wide, slow vibrato in even eighths. (It helps to have your eyes at half-mast, preferably as the result of drinking two bottles of champagne.) Arranged as Kiss often did, the guitars here are doubled (and their vibrato is closely matched), but note how they diverge to create a harmony in the last bar. *On the CD: A basic rhythm track, à la Paul Stanley, is heard beneath this example.*

Ex. 2

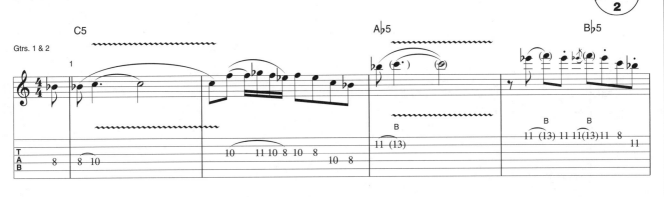

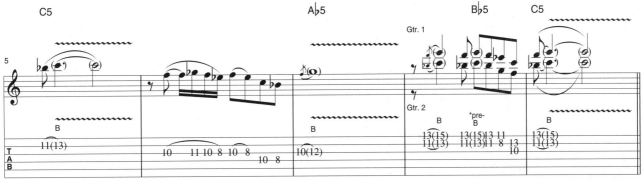

*Both notes pre-bent from previous fret position.

When Kiss really turned on the heavy, Ace could make the most of a slow part. In **Ex. 3**, fills are played between a basic rock pattern of *F#5* to *A5*. To get the hiccuping cluck into the first fill, strike the adjacent lower string—muted—before sounding your target note. For example, mute the 4th string with a downstroke from your picking hand's thumb before continuing the downstroke for the first *C#* on the 3rd string—it's like you're arpeggiating the two strings very slowly. The right-hand positioning sets up squeal harmonics when the lick is heard again in bar 3. Slight bends on each note keep it from sounding flat. For the last lick, an *F#* blues descent, pick every note after the initial 16th-note triplet.

Ex. 3

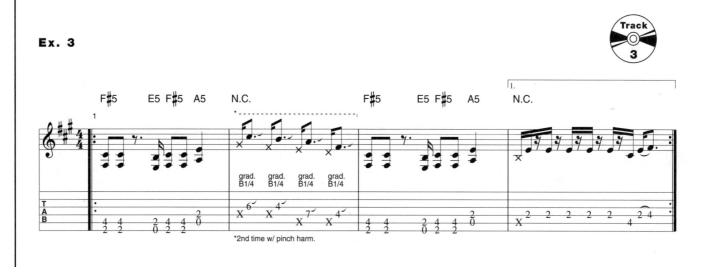

Over the course of **Ex. 4** a solo picks up momentum. It's all right out of *G* pentatonic minor and *G* blues, with wide bends on the 2nd and 3rd strings—with the exception of the quick chromatic passages, which are delivered for a slur effect within the blues box. Then we're in the same box but up an octave for a classic rock lick. There is no shortage of rockers who love this phrase, with its bent 3rd string and mid-lick pull-offs that make for fleet-sounding fingers. Ace also loved the way this lick cycled; see how it comes around on a different beat each time it repeats. As elsewhere, Ace here is very Page-like.

Ex. 4

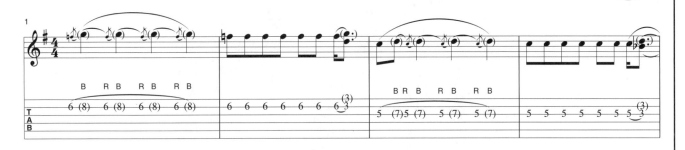

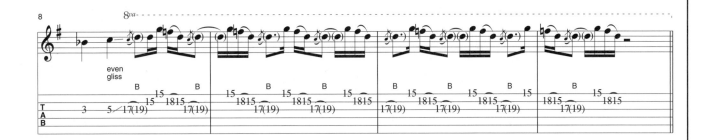

CHAPTER 2
Angus Young of AC/DC

Australian bands became the rage in America when record companies latched onto them and started importing them cheaply in the late 1970s and early '80s. But only one has had both a lasting effect on hard rock and significant staying power: AC/DC. Led by guitarist Angus Young for more than 30 years, the band has inspired more power-chord thundering and head-banging than any group since Led Zeppelin. Propelled by Young's riffing and the steady rhythm playing of brother Malcolm, the band continues to deliver sledgehammer-quality rock in a formula that hasn't changed for decades. The only thing that differentiates AC/DC now from its humble beginnings back in the 1970s is its lead singer—and that's because the first one made the mistake of dying just as the band was breaking through in the U.S. But it's Angus Young's Gibson SG that still powers the band, which has come to stand for hard rock for the last 30 years.

BIOGRAPHY

Angus Young was born on March 31, 1955, in Glasgow, Scotland. When he was eight years old, his family moved to Australia. The family was musical from top to bottom; Angus's oldest brother George was a member of the Easybeats, Australia's answer to the Beatles. And brother Malcolm, two years older than Angus, had an early affinity for the guitar. In a magnanimous display of brotherly love, Malcolm eventually gave Angus a discarded Hofner to play. Spurning lessons, Angus learned from his brothers, and George's success inspired both Malcolm and Angus to master the instrument. When George returned home after the demise of the Easybeats, he put both Angus and Malcolm in the studio and recorded them as part of his own album project.

Barely 15, young Angus quit school (at the legal minimum age allowed by Australian law) and went on to work as a printer at a pornography magazine called *Ribald*. He formed a band called Tantrum—and purchased an SG, which suited his small frame—while Malcolm formed the Velvet Underground, a group that would forever be confused with the same-named New York art-punk band. The Velvet Underground didn't last long—maybe it was the name—and Malcolm then dreamed up AC/DC, named after the electrical marking he saw on a vacuum cleaner. He imagined a group that was equal parts glam and British blues, perhaps with a keyboard player. But he realized the band needed something more visceral, and he turned to younger brother Angus to add guitar to the sound.

After mixing and matching various singers and rhythm sections, the Young brothers formalized AC/DC in 1974. They enlisted Bon Scott as their singer, a man whose gargled-granite vocals were as rough and crusty as his lifestyle. Together, they perfected a simple brand of brutal rock in the similarly brutal clubs of Sydney, where audiences were known to pummel bands they didn't like. AC/DC came through unscathed, developing a frenetic live show that was, if anything, more crazed than their Australian fans. Angus raced across Aussie stages like a puppet on the wrong end of a stun gun, jerking so maniacally that he appeared on the verge of shaking his head and limbs from his body.

After a year of honing their sound, AC/DC released their debut record in 1975. Produced by eldest brother George, *High Voltage* set the tone for the band's career, built on simple chord progressions, repeated riffs, and amps cranked well past the point of safe listening. The Youngs also had a knack for catchy, stadium-style lyrics and salacious double entendres, which instantly won them legions of testosterone-fueled male fans. Angus's attire, that of a prep school lad clad in cap and knickers, only reinforced the image of schoolboys bent on partying until something went seriously out of control.

Following *High Voltage* with *TNT* in 1976, and then a year later with *Let There Be*

Rock, the band began to gain a following in the U.K. The success of 1978's *Powerage* in Europe and Australia convinced Atlantic Records to give AC/DC a push in the United States. With the release of *Highway to Hell* in 1979, American audiences finally fell prey to the AC/DC juggernaut. Produced by Robert John "Mutt" Lange (who would later become Mr. Shania Twain and gain well-deserved fame for producing Def Leppard's *Pyromania*), the album was nearly violent in its volume and featured the in-your-face title track as well as "Touch Too Much" and "Girls Got Rhythm." American radio quickly picked up on the band, and suddenly AC/DC was the newest international darling of hard rock.

Anticipation over their next album ran high, right up until the moment that Bon Scott was found dead in his car of an alcohol overdose in February 1980. Almost everyone wrote the band off, believing that Bon Scott's brand of sterility-inducing vocals was irreplaceable. But the Young brothers persevered, finding a new singer in Brian Johnson, an unknown who had performed with the British band Geordie. Johnson's vocal style was, if anything, even more ferocious than Scott's, and he and the boys spent the summer working on the aptly titled *Back in Black*.

Back in Black defied all expectations. Not only were the songs more raucous and sonically interesting than anything else the band had ever recorded, but the AC/DC formula also got a facelift. Songs like "Shoot to Thrill" and the title cut featured blistering layers of guitar, while dirge-like tracks such as "Hell's Bells" showed that the band could rumble at low speeds like an idling 18-wheeler. Then and now considered a hard rock masterpiece, the album became one of the best-selling records of all time.

AC/DC followed up with the posthumous American release of the Bon Scott album *Dirty Deeds Done Dirt Cheap* (it had previously been available only in Australia and the U.K.) and then *For Those About to Rock*, two guitar slabfests that mined the same guitar vein as *Back in Black*. Each of the title tunes became rock radio staples, further cementing the band's reputation as the leading purveyors of unadorned hard rock. The records may have been formulaic, but since AC/DC concocted the formula itself, no one was complaining.

Since then, AC/DC has released a slew of albums, all of which have featured anthemic cuts ("Who Made Who," "Thunderstruck," "Heatseeker") built on Angus's simple riffs, ear-shattering volume, and knack for twisting the basic blues box into yet another uniquely identifiable AC/DC tune. The albums have varied in originality, though, with some—like *Fly on the Wall*—sounding like retreads. Yet the continued success is a testament to AC/DC's choice of consistency over complexity. The band successfully competed with, and has largely outlived, a generation of heavy metal shredders and speed metal freaks that have all but disappeared.

While the formula has worn thin to casual listeners over the last decade, it hasn't stopped hardcore fans and hard rock aficionados from buying records and devouring concert tickets. The band remains a concert draw to this day, with Brian Johnson finally outliving the "new guy" tag, having been in the band for nearly a quarter-century longer than Bon Scott was. And Angus hasn't outgrown his knickers nor his knack for serving up riffs that have the strength and staying power of cast iron.

GEAR & SETUP

Angus is identified with one guitar and one guitar only: the Gibson SG. He owns as many as two dozen and still has the very first one he ever bought, a '68. His favorites now include models from 1964 though 1981, especially 1967–68. Several have the tremolo arm that was only occasionally popular on early SGs. The model has become so associated with Angus that Gibson introduced the Angus Young Signature SG in 2000. The pickups in his guitars, Angus Young Signature humbuckers, are also tailored to his sound.

His strings are Ernie Ball Super Slinkys gauged .009–.042. To make sure he's hitting them with everything he can, he uses extra-heavy 121mm picks.

Like the vast majority of hard rock guitarists, Young uses Marshalls. His basic setup includes four Marshall 1959 SLP 100-watt heads. These are reissues of the Super Lead "Plexi" Marshalls made in the late 1960s and early '70s. Each head powers two 4x12 cabs. Onstage he adds a Marshall JTM45 head that's run into one

CHECKLIST ✓

Guitar . . . . Gibson SG	**Tone** . . . . Thick, all tone pots on full
Setup . . . . Standard	**Picking** . . . . Hard
Strings . . . . Ernie Ball Super Slinkys	**Attack** . . . . Harder
Pickups . . . . Stock	**Signature traits** . . . . Heavy riffs, pull-offs
Amplification . . . Marshall 1959 SLP 100, 4x12 cabinets	**Influences** . . . . . . Chuck Berry, Keith Richards, Elmore James
Settings . . . . Volume high, but not saturating the amp	**Overall approach** . . . . Brutal and volatile
Effects . . . . None	

SELECTED DISCOGRAPHY

High Voltage (Atco, 1976)
Let There Be Rock (Atco, 1977)
Powerage (Atlantic, 1978)
Highway to Hell (Epic, 1979)
Back in Black (Atlantic, 1980)
Dirty Deeds Done Dirt Cheap (Atlantic, 1975; released in the U.S. in 1981)
For Those About to Rock (Atlantic, 1981)
Who Made Who soundtrack (Atlantic, 1986)
Blow Up Your Video (Atlantic, 1988)
The Razor's Edge (Atco, 1990)
Ballbreaker (EastWest, 1995)

RECOMMENDED CUTS

"T.N.T." (*High Voltage*)
"Touch Too Much" (*Highway to Hell*)
"Dirty Deeds Done Dirt Cheap" (*Dirty Deeds Done Dirt Cheap*)
"Back in Black" (*Back in Black*)
"Hell's Bells" (*Back in Black*)
"Shoot to Thrill" (*Back in Black*)
"Whole Lotta Rosie" (*Let There Be Rock*)
"You Shook Me All Night Long" (*Back in Black*)
"Highway to Hell" (*Highway to Hell*)
"Thunderstruck" (*The Razor's Edge*)
"For Those About to Rock (We Salute You)" (*For Those About to Rock*)
"Who Made Who" (*Who Made Who*)
"Heatseeker" (*Blow Up Your Video*)

4x12 cab and then through an isolation box that is sent to the front of house for blending into the master mix. Onstage he also uses a Samson UR-5 wireless system.

Young uses no effects at all. In fact, he claims that his sound is quite clean when recording and that the distortion comes naturally from the guitars and amps.

That's it. Nothing else. Nada. Zip. Zilch. Everything else comes from Angus and his ten fingers. A "Whole Lotta Rosie" indeed.

STYLE & TECHNIQUE

With Gibson SG in hand and Marshall amp cranked to at least 10, Angus Young created a style that launched a thousand hard rock bands over the last two decades. Even today, few can make it sound as pure as he can. Ace Frehley had a similarly stripped-down style, but he relied more heavily on the interplay with the rest of the band, whereas Young's sound *is* the band—even more so than the gasping-for-air vocals of his lead singers. From the opening notes of everything from "TNT" to "Thunderstruck," an AC/DC song is one of the most identifiable of all hard rock sounds.

It's nearly impossible to describe Angus's playing without overcomplicating it. There's a certain surgical rigidity to his guitar work that is almost militaristic in its cadence and simplicity. It's a form of controlled violence—repeated punching, a heavy attack, and no frills to tart things up. In fact, trying to eliminate any and all flourishes from one's playing is the best way to emulate an Angus riff. Though he does manage to find his own groove in simple 4/4 pieces, it's more about making the bombast resonate with the listener than it is about having them get caught up in the moment. (This is, after all, the quintessential headbanging band.) A heavy pick delivers his bruising attack both in riffs and solos; indeed, a powerful right hand is a requirement in making sure the strings know they're being savaged.

The distinctive element that Angus manages to convey in his playing is taste. If it weren't for Young's restraint and taste—which help make his songs such catchy pieces of music—AC/DC songs might otherwise be the kind of by-the-numbers tunes easily peddled by any hard rock band.

Amazingly, Angus makes do with two, three, or four notes per riff—or even per solo. This has precedence in the British Invasion, but from a band few would consider a forebear of AC/DC: the Kinks. The Kinks pioneered simple yet heavy repetition ("You Really Got Me," "All the Day and All of the Night"), never veering far from the root to create a mesmerizing riff. Like the Kinks—and unlike Eric Clapton, Jimmy Page, Ritchie Blackmore, or even Black Sabbath's Tony Iommi—Angus kept himself pretty well locked into the blues box, finding a seemingly endless number of ways to recycle the same handful of notes.

As we've noted, it would be easy to dismiss Angus's style as formulaic, but that would overlook the fact that it's *his* formula. When you hear someone else doing it, they're copying the Angus concoction. And it works better for him than anyone else. He manages to take the simplest of traditional patterns and make them sound uniquely and originally his (something perhaps equaled only by Iommi and Blackmore). He also is unique in making mountains out of cowboy-chord molehills. Nobody gets more meat out of open-position chords than he does. Maybe that's why they call him "Angus."

Angus gives much of the credit for AC/DC's groove to his brother Malcolm, who holds down the basic rhythm chores and keeps the band on track. Angus says that his role as lead guitarist is to add color to the songs, although that understates his contribution by a huge margin. The band is driven by Angus's signature riffs as well as his readily identifiable soloing style.

Young's solos never veer out of blues basics, although his aggressiveness gives those solos a ferocity few other guitarists can muster. Angus's most notable solo technique are his hard-won bends and a style of rapid trilling that predates Eddie Van Halen's fretboard tapping by several years. When done correctly, it sounds very similar to Van Halen's tapping, but Young does it by spreading pull-offs (and the attendant hammer-ons) across several frets. He achieves his vibrato with his fingers, not his wrist, utilizing the strength of fingers behind the fretted note to bend strings upwards.

LESSON

When you listen carefully to Angus's tone, you'll hear that it's not very distorted, even though it's louder than God. To cop the sound, set your guitar volume around 7 and the amp's gain around 4; alternately, you could use more volume on your guitar (near 10) and less gain on the amp (near 2). The goal is to push the amp past clean but not to the point of saturation. That's how Angus lets all the notes in his chords come through clearly (if not cleanly) while still delivering them with a sharp kick in the knickers. That's made plain in Angus parts like **Ex. 1**, where the guitar's settings aren't changed at all between the ominous arpeggiated measures at the opening and the power chords that follow. It's central to Angus's approach that those power chords are played in open position.

Ex. 1

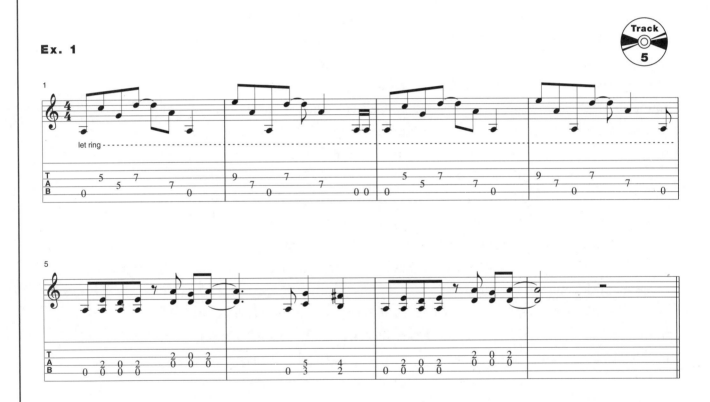

Here's the other Angus riff (**Ex. 2**). Again we're using open-position chord voicings (though Malcolm would often mirror the changes in barre chords), broken up by a quick lick. There are two things to know about hitting this lick right. First, you have to pick each of those first four notes; it's tempting to pull off to the open strings, but you won't get the power or volume you need from each note. Second, that's a full bend on the 3rd-string A. Respect the bend—it's quick, but get all the way up to B and back.

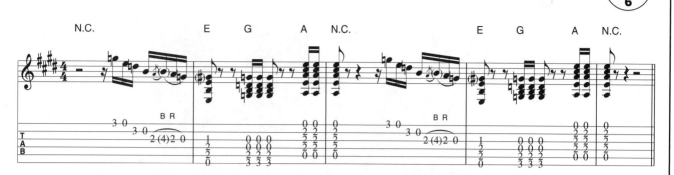

Ex. 2

While AC/DC might not sound much like a blues band, Angus does wear his heart on his sleeve when it comes to solo time. **Example 3**'s solo of punchy riffs and rapid vibrato has more to do with Buddy Guy than with any rock influence. Angus manages to avoid blues clichés in his melodic lines, and he gives his solos a nice punch by being right in the rhythm pocket. As usual, his sound is dry as a bone and his vibrato is rapid. If you can't make it, don't fake it.

Ex. 3

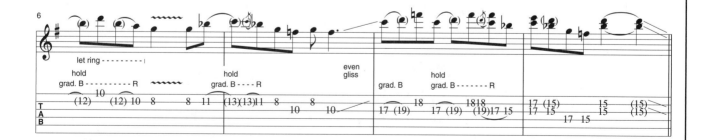

CHAPTER 3
Eddie Van Halen

Eddie Van Halen is the most influential and important hard rock guitarist since the days of Hendrix, Page, Clapton, and Beck. Not only did he bring a completely new approach to the instrument, he saved an entire generation of guitarists from the horror of disco and synthesized music. To listen to Van Halen the first time was to hear electric guitar playing reinvented. To listen to him again was to hear a player who seemed to have an endless supply of skills and new techniques for each succeeding album. The fact that he still inspires guitarists more than a quarter-century later is something very few musicians of any era can claim.

BIOGRAPHY

Edward Van Halen was born on January 26, 1955, in Nijmegan, Netherlands. His family, including older brother Alex, moved to Southern California in 1967. Both he and his brother took classical piano lessons as children, but they soon abandoned those studies in favor of rock 'n' roll. Originally, Alex played guitar and Eddie played drums—until they realized that neither of them was very good at his respective instrument. When he decided to switch to guitar while Alex sat down at the drums, Eddie Van Halen set himself on a course that can only be described as fated.

The two brothers, inspired by British rock, were quick to form local rock bands. Eddie, in particular, was influenced by Eric Clapton's nuanced yet heavy approach to the guitar. Clapton was at the height of his fame, having found renown in John Mayall's Bluesbreakers, the Yardbirds, and Cream.

Like thousands of kids in the early '70s, the Van Halen brothers played in one local band after another, none of which attracted any attention until they met aspiring singer David Lee Roth. Playing in a band called Mammoth with bass player Michael Anthony, they ultimately hooked up with Roth, whose caché was increased by having a PA system and a place to practice.

Adopting the name Van Halen, the band bombarded the Pasadena party circuit before strafing the Sunset Strip in a series of non-stop bookings that made them the pre-eminent attraction on that hallowed musical ground. (VH's stint on the Strip would pave the way for later hard rock and hair-metal bands to hone their chops in front of enthusiastic crowds, willing groupies, and interested label execs.) That led to opening spots in L.A. for marquee groups like Kiss. Impressed with the band's talent, Kiss executive and bassist Gene Simmons paid for their first big demo, but no one stepped up to offer the band a contract.

The constant slogging through the club world did eventually garner label attention—by this time, they were impossible to miss—and VH signed with Warner Bros. in 1977. The band blitzkrieged its way through the studio, recording dozens of songs (with very little overdubbing) before stripping back to what would be their 1978 debut, *Van Halen*.

Everything about the record was over-the-top and technically brilliant. No one had heard the kind of extreme guitar playing that Eddie whipped out on "Runnin' with the Devil," "Ain't Talkin' 'Bout Love," and most notably "Eruption," arguably the most stunning display of solo electric guitar ever put on record. With whammy-bar screeches and impossibly fast finger-tapped runs, Van Halen displayed unparalleled virtuosity, especially for a guy in his early 20s. Beyond that, most guitarists had no idea how he played the way he did—or even what he was actually doing.

The band went on tour, and, propelled by its cover of the Kinks' "You Really Got Me," the album took off. They followed up with *Van Halen II* in 1979, an album that showed the band in full cock-rock mode, featuring more of Roth's tongue-in-cheek sexuality and even more of Eddie's full frontal assault on the guitar. This time he came up with bulldozer riffs like "D.O.A." and "Light Up the Sky," the latter featuring a blistering solo that would set the bar for a whole generation of shredders

(EVH was in no way a shredder; more than most guitarists, he knew when to down-shift). He also transmogrified "Eruption" into an acoustic guitar masterpiece by applying the same double-handed tapping to the instrumental "Spanish Fly." It was one of the few acoustic moments in what would be a very long electric career.

Every subsequent album and tour solidified the band's appeal until they became the undisputed arena draw in the U.S. Their third album, 1980's *Women and Children First*, was a departure from the previous two and showcased Van Halen's ability to play swaggering blues ("Take Your Whiskey Home") and full-throttle boogie ("Loss of Control"). There was a jaw-dropping guitar intro to "Everybody Wants Some" which resembled nothing so much as the outraged death screeches of dinosaurs, as well as the piano-driven "And the Cradle Will Rock" (which many listeners still think is played on guitar).

With its fourth album, 1981's *Fair Warning*, the band veered away from "all partying, all the time" toward something significantly more visceral, dark, and disturbing. An overlooked masterpiece, *Fair Warning* grabbed listeners by the throat from the vicious opening taps of "Mean Street" to the phase-shifted scorching of "Hear About It Later." In between were the requisite VH laboratory creations like "Sunday Afternoon in the Park" and the radio ass-kicker "Unchained." Observers looked at the record as Eddie's attempt to pull the band to a more sophisticated musical level, but he lost the ongoing tug-of-war with Roth by the time the next record, *Diver Down*, was released in 1982. An album that clocked in at barely half an hour long, it was primarily a set of cover tunes that gave Roth an opportunity to indulge in his best vaudeville shtick. Yet Eddie saved the album with the truly inspired "Little Guitars," which featured harmonic tapping; the ethereal "Cathedral" with its rapid-fire volume-knob swells; and the horror-show instrumental "Intrusion."

Even as the band started to fray around the edges from David and Eddie's increasing personal friction, it continued to rule the arenas and set the standard for hard rock worldwide. Eddie took some time off to record the solo to Michael Jackson's "Beat It," resulting in more mainstream exposure for the guitarist, who could now be heard tapping on just about every record player and radio in the United States. Van Halen—the band—managed to do the improbable; it topped its previous records with the release in 1984 of the album *1984*. The record was the ultimate result of the band's push/pull: It had Roth's burlesque humor coupled with Eddie's tougher musical edge. From "Panama" and "Hot for Teacher" to "Girl Gone Bad" and "House of Pain," the album didn't have a single song that wasn't brilliantly crafted, constructed, and produced. It was as if both Roth and EVH had forced as much of themselves into each piece as possible, until the result was quintessential Van Halen.

Having put everything they had into the creation of *1984*, it appeared there was nowhere left for Roth and Eddie to go—except their separate ways. Roth put out a solo record and then left the band, claiming he was fired. Eddie claimed that Roth quit because he didn't want to commit to the band full-time. Regardless, the first and finest Van Halen era was over.

The three remaining members of Van Halen then brought in Sammy Hagar, the "Red Rocker" vocalist best known for boxing-themed shows and the hit "I Can't Drive 55." The first effort of Van Halen 2.0 was 1986's *5150* (the name taken from the LAPD police code for a psycho on the loose). The opening cut, "Good Enough," featured Hagar doing his best Roth impersonation, but it only took a few listens to hear that this wasn't going to be same VH. Gone were Roth's double entendres and humor, replaced by Hagar's drunken frat-boy catcalling. Eddie's playing, as always, was still eye-popping, but the songs themselves were more pop-oriented, a little less inventive, and produced with an ear toward mainstream radio airplay. The formula worked—*5150* became the band's best-selling record. Buyers ate up the lighter version of VH, which from this point forward would feature more Eddie on keyboards and more Sammy on guitar. It would also mark a series of cutesy album titles (*OU812* in 1988 and *For Unlawful Carnal Knowledge* in 1991). The albums sold very well, but diehard fans were disenchanted. It was clear that Hagar was leading Van Halen toward the middle of the road and away from cutting-edge hard rock.

CHECKLIST ✓

Guitars . . . . Homemade; Peavey Wolfgang

Setup . . . . Standard

Strings 009–.042

Pickups . . . . Seymour Duncan, Gibson PAFs

Amplification . . . Marshall 100-watt Super Lead "Plexi," Peavey 5150

Settings . . . . Maxed

Effects . . . . MXR Phase 90 Phaser, MXR Stereo Flanger, Maestro Echoplex

Tone . . . . Hot and smooth, like controlled burning

Attack . . . . Whatever it takes, from every angle

Signature traits . . . . Two-handed tapping, whammy-bar dive bombs, active rhythm parts

Influences . . . . . . Eric Clapton

Overall approach . . . . Keep it interesting and keep experimenting

SELECTED DISCOGRAPHY

(all on Warner Bros.)
Van Halen (1978)
Van Halen II (1979)
Women and Children First (1980)
Fair Warning (1981)
Diver Down (1982)
1984 (1984)
5150 (1986)
OU812 (1988)
For Unlawful Carnal Knowledge (1991)
Live: Right Here, Right Now (1993)
Balance (1995)

RECOMMENDED CUTS

"Eruption" (*Van Halen*)
"Ain't Talkin' 'Bout Love" (*Van Halen*)
"D.O.A." (*Van Halen II*)
"Light Up the Sky" (*Van Halen II*)
"Spanish Fly" (*Van Halen II*)
"Mean Streets" (*Fair Warning*)
"Unchained" (*Fair Warning*)
"Hear About It Later" (*Fair Warning*)
"Little Guitars" (*Diver Down*)
"Top Jimmy" (*1984*)
"Cathedral" (*Diver Down*)
"Panama" (*1984*)
"House of Pain" (*1984*)
"Humans Being" (*Best of Van Halen, Vol. 1*, Warner Bros.)

It didn't help that Eddie's personal life was now tabloid news, from marital problems with his wife, actress Valerie Bertinelli, to his battle with alcohol and the birth of his son Wolfgang. The band carried on, releasing an uninspired live album in 1993 and *Balance* in 1995. Eddie seemed to have regained his groove when he contributed the song "Humans Being" to the *Twister* soundtrack. The song would have fit in perfectly with *Fair Warning*, and featured an extended solo of pure genius. It seemed like the old Van Halen was back—until Hagar found himself out of the band. Like Roth before him, the explanations were murky. Eddie claimed that Hagar didn't want to commit to rehearsals and touring, while Hagar claimed that Eddie fired him for leaving on a Hawaiian vacation before "Humans Being" was completed (many of the vocal tracks are actually Eddie).

Eddie and Roth made a stab at reconciliation, a union that lasted long enough for one MTV appearance, a couple of new songs, and a greatest-hits record. Then they started feuding publicly, and Eddie went looking for someone new. His manager, who also managed Extreme, suggested Extreme's Gary Cherone, and Eddie fell for it. The result was the album *Van Halen III*, about which the less said the better.

Drained from so much public bickering, Eddie took time off to try and get his personal life straightened out. He received treatment for tongue cancer, got sober, and had his hip replaced. Although his marriage broke up, he touted the value of fatherhood and seemed to be perennially working on some solo project. That all changed in early 2004, when he and Hagar kissed and made up and announced a summer tour, to be followed by a new album. In anticipation of the tour, the remastered compilation *Best of Both Worlds* was released, forcing fans to imagine Roth and Hagar on the same stage while Cherone weeps backstage anonymously.

Diehards hoping to get Roth and Eddie back on stage moaned, but the reality was that any Eddie Van Halen was a lot better than none at all. Eddie has, quite simply, become the most important guitarist of the past three decades. Scrutinized and studied on a par with only Jimi Hendrix, he has contributed more as an innovative guitarist to the genre of hard rock than anyone else. (Hendrix's contributions were broader and less specific to hard rock.) Eddie's songs have been models of songwriting simplicity—often consisting of only two or three chords—while his playing has fleshed out the sparse changes with levels of complexity and ornamentation from taps and squeals to whammy-bar dives. He takes the simple and pulls everything out of it that can be gotten, especially things that no other guitarist would have ever considered. Therein lies his genius.

GEAR & SETUP

Perhaps no other guitarist's gear has been so thoroughly analyzed as Eddie Van Halen's. But guitarists trying to emulate his sound have heard Eddie say it's all in the fingers—he gets his famous "brown sound" no matter which, or whose, setup he's using.

His early guitars included both Gibson Les Pauls and Fender Stratocasters. But he found the sound of the Strat—which he used for its Fender whammy bar—to be too thin. So he shoved a PAF pickup into a Strat-style body to give it a fatter Les Paul–like sound. Then he added one of Floyd Rose's first locking trem units, installed an unfinished neck, and created a guitar later known as "Frankenstein." This is the striped axe (the first stripes on Frankenstein were bicycle tape, not paint) featured on his early albums. Many of his guitars during the late '70s and early '80s were cobbled together from spare parts, with a popular combo being a Charvel body and a Kramer neck.

Based on his success with Kramer necks, he endorsed a line of their guitars for a while but soon began cannibalizing these as well, using Seymour Duncan pickups, the Floyd Rose trem, and other mechanical parts. The Floyd Roses were always mounted flush with the body so they could only be lowered and not pulled up. He also took to using a Steinberger TransTrem on his guitars so that he could change the pitch across all the strings at once.

Nonetheless, Eddie employed quite an array of other guitars that weren't home-made concoctions. These included several Stratocasters and Telecasters, a '58 Gibson Flying V, and an Ibanez Destroyer (although he did hack that one up with a chainsaw; it's on view on the cover of *Women and Children First*).

Eddie messed around with his guitars' electronics extensively. He was known to rewire pickup coils, dampen their vibrations with wax, and remove the tone controls, leaving only a working volume knob. He also mounted the pickups to the body, not the pickguard (even when they appear to be "on" the pickguard, they are routed through the plastic and into the body cavity), so that they would vibrate in sympathy with the guitar's solid wood.

Constantly looking for a better guitar, he joined with Ernie Ball/Music Man in 1991 to produce the EVH signature guitar. That relationship turned sour (Eddie claimed there were quality issues), and he went to the maker of his 5150 amps, Peavey, to start a new line of guitars known as the Wolfgang. He still uses those today, with modifications (including a bridge lever he developed to drop the low E string a whole-step).

Despite claims to the contrary, Eddie relied almost exclusively on Marshall 100-watt "Plexi" Super Leads going through 4x12 cabinets for most of the Roth-era recordings. Live, he would use newer Marshalls, often in a pair with one modified using various voltage converters; by lowering the voltage by about 10 volts, EVH could get the classic Marshall tone of an overdriven power-amp stage at a lower volume, and more reliably. Plus, he was changing tubes every week, and varying the voltage helped preserve tube and amp life. Around 1991 he started using Soldanos, then worked with Peavey to create the 5150 line of amps. The original version is a two-channel amp (for distortion and clean sounds), and the 5150 II is a three-channel amp that adds a "crunch" channel. The main thing to consider about his amp settings is that, in both the studio and live, they are run as hot and as loud as possible.

Eddie's early effects were primarily floor pedals, notably the small MXR boxes attached to his homemade pedalboard. He got an incredible amount of mileage out of phase-shifting and digital delay, along with using some nice distortion boxes. His sound over the years has been built on the MXR Phase 90 Phaser, MXR Stereo Flanger, Maestro Echoplex (which he housed in an old WWII bombshell), Univox EC-80 Echo, Boss SD-1 Super Overdrive, Boss OC-2 Octave Divider, and Dunlop Crybaby wah pedal. Later on he added upscale and rackmount effects such as Eventide's H3000 Harmonizer and the Lexicon PCM 70 Stereo Reverb.

His strings are on the light side, usually .009–.042 sets, and Eddie always uses a heavy pick—rarely does he use his fingers other than in the occasional pick-and-fingers combo.

STYLE & TECHNIQUE

While you can overanalyze the simplicity of a player like Angus Young, you can never, never overanalyze Van Halen's playing—unless you ask Eddie, who is always at a loss to describe his skills. His two-handed tapping alone is a technique that can—and has—taken up entire books. Although Eddie wasn't the first to tap the fretboard with his right hand (guitarists like Harvey Mandel and Genesis' Steve Hackett had done it in a limited fashion before), no one else had used it as the foundation for entire solos or musical passages. The same is true of his hammer-on/pull-off style, which was applied sparingly by guitarists such as Angus Young and Allan Holdsworth. In Van Halen's hands, it became a technique that was almost as multifunctional as strumming.

What a lot of people missed about his tapping was that it was never employed just for tapping's sake, "Eruption" aside. EVH legitimately incorporated the technique into his solos and fills as a faster way of getting from point A to point Z; the majority of his longer tapping sequences serve the purpose of transitioning between registers. Countless guitarists have shut themselves off in the woodshed to master tapping, but it's essentially about drumming on the strings with your fingers. If you approach it like you do drumming fingers on a table—16th- and 32nd-notes come a lot faster when you get more fingers involved—you'll be on your way to tapping with a good sense of time. Perhaps Eddie's early days on drums had some influence on his tap technique.

Eddie's tapping came in many forms, including a single note dropped from above into an otherwise conventionally fretted line. While other players were picking up on the basics, Eddie was on to the next thing, such as actually bending a tapped note with his right-hand forefinger (be ready for calluses where you haven't had them before). When he wanted vibrato on a tapped note, he simply shook a fretted *left-hand* note while the right-handed tap sat in place. There are examples of him tapping with clean tone (even on acoustics and nylon-string guitars), but anyone would find it easier to get started with a healthy dose of overdrive.

There are other aspects of his playing that bear close examination. He is a monster rhythm player, and his ability to insert fills and play variations of chord progressions—almost as if he were soloing each chord instead of simply playing it—is one of his most distinctive yet unheralded traits. Playing the only polyphonic instrument in the band, Eddie had a lot of space to fill, and his rhythm approach is on a par with some of the finest jazz comping (active rhythm playing with alternate chord voicings and transitional phrases).

His finishing touches—including pinch harmonics, quick taps, and a shuddering whammy-bar-induced vibrato—always keep his playing interesting as he doses each song, and indeed each verse, with a different set of ornaments. It's common for him to combine these nonconventional techniques, too: He'll hit a pinch harmonic and then bend the note up a step and a half; he'll roll back the volume, depress the whammy bar, and then touch a double-stop harmonic as the whammy bar and the volume come up simultaneously.

Rarely will he play two verses in a row with the same voicings or ornaments; the only thing that remains constant is the chord change, which is often back and forth between only two chords. Van Halen riffs tend to be fundamentally simplistic, often echoing the double-stop riffs of ZZ Top or Deep Purple. But Eddie's knack for revoicing chord changes, playing partial chords, arpeggiating, and keeping his parts in perpetual motion makes even the simplest changes and riffs exciting.

He was one of the first rock guitarists to take advantage of technical improvements to the whammy bar (previously known as a tremolo bar or arm). Unlike their predecessors, the Floyd Rose and Kahler units stayed in tune no matter how much they were abused. Van Halen's style incorporated the whammy as both a subtle vibrato effect and as a dive-bombing harridan wail. It's important to point out that Eddie never pulled up on the bar—he always pushed down or let it rise from a depressed position to get an upward shriek. This being the case, he mounts his trems with no float.

EVH has detuned often, either a half- or whole-step, and he likes dropped-*D* enough to have developed a *D* lever for his Peavey's bridge. Nonetheless, there are very few examples of alternate tuning in his catalog. "Top Jimmy" (*DADACD*) is one exception.

LESSON

Van Halen's guitar style can be intimidating, but spend some time and you'll find that his techniques aren't out of reach. Mind you, just because you go to church now and then doesn't mean you know how to walk on water.

Still, it's worth a try. Let's start at the bottom, with Eddie's rhythm parts. While he has the capability to comp like a jazz player, he knows when to stick to a simple riff. In **Ex. 1** the riff picks up a lot of bottom end and doesn't show any flash until the quick fill at the end of bar 3 before the change to *B* minor. A little glimpse of speed, like this one, keeps the part moving and interesting.

Ex. 1

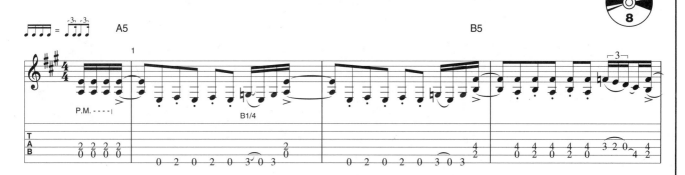

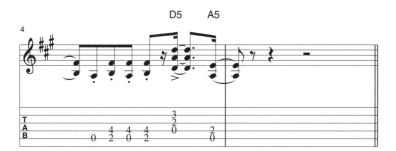

Example 2 starts with another simple rhythm part, then gets interesting real fast with a rapid and rolling fill. While there are a ton of cool VH riffs, the really good stuff is what Eddie does in between them. Like a great donut, it's all in the filling.

There are a couple things worth noting about the simple rhythm part. Eddie often downstrokes very hard, which, with the benefit of a cranked-to-overdrive amp, allows for lots of overtones. Notice how overtones creep into the palm-muted *G*'s; get some thumb flesh into the picking hand to help bring out the false harmonic. Leaving your finger gently poised over the same position for the choked strokes lets another harmonic come through. It keeps the part fun.

The rapid fill starts with a pinched harmonic bend (a full step and a half, which actually isn't too tough on the 3rd string in that position). Pinch harmonics are achieved with the picking hand. Pluck the string with the edge of the pick (just a sliver) and the edge of your thumb almost at the same time. As the pick releases the string, it hits the flesh of your thumb, producing a harmonic. Make sure the thumb doesn't mute the note; if it does, try moving your picking hand to other positions over the string to find the harmonic.

While the harmony of the line seems rudderless above the rhythm, notice that it outlines an *F#m* arpeggio. It's clever on Ed's part: If you played an *F#m* chord where he plays the lick, you'll see that it makes a nice passing or intermediary chord.

Link the rhythm and fill parts together as seamlessly as possible.

Ex. 2

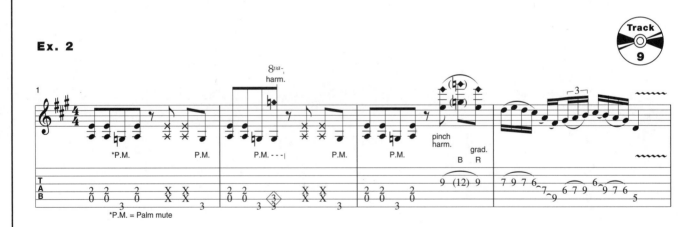

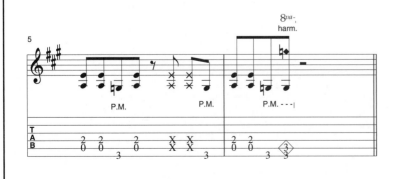

Time to tap. As mentioned above, there are no empty-headed tap runs in EVH's catalog. The opening taps in **Ex. 3** are merely a rev-up to the hanging and bended taps that sing the ear-tilting melody. Coming in sets of three, the tap pattern is a common one: tap high note, pull off to left-hand note, then hammer on. An often overlooked aspect of tapping is muting. Let some of the meat of your right hand (or even your right arm) mute the strings a bit behind the tap or else you'll get ringing strings that muddle the passage.

The next tap type heard (going into the second measure) is similar, but you hang on the tapped note and pull it up a step. Bend a full step, in kind, on the left-hand fretted notes, so that when you pull off, the fretted note gets the bend down. Let the time go loose, and when you sustain on that last tapped note, add some vibrato with the *fretted* note behind it.

Ex. 3

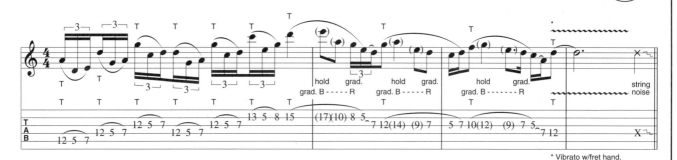

* Vibrato w/fret hand.

There are many unconventional techniques in Eddie's bag of tricks. Check out Ex. 4, which is our Whitman's Sampler of EVH licks. On the CD each is heard twice, with a bar of lead-in time.

The first example contains two single-note taps—those oddball high notes that seem to drop in from nowhere. Both are in the blues scale and could just as easily be fretted in position, but the taps give them a much cooler attack and delivery.

Second is a pinch harmonic on a low *A* (6th string, 5th fret). Begin with your pick in normal position, and as you pinch each pair of notes, bring your hand a bit closer to the neck each time. Check in advance to find your guitar's ideal spots for catching overtones.

The third nugget sounds crazy but it's not hard. It consists of taps, grouped in threes. The muting behind the string (in this case, done with the forearm) is lifted after the first barrage, and the gradual lift makes for a swelling sound.

Last is a pinch harmonic treated to some whammy action. Have fun with this stuff. Eddie always seemed to be wearing a grin.

Ex. 4

*Tap pre-bent note at 15th fret.

pitches: E E C♯ C♯ A A E

*Pinch each pair of harm. closer to neck.

CHAPTER 4
Dave Navarro

Nobody steered alternative rock more aggressively into the realm of hard rock than Dave Navarro. From the opening chords of the first Jane's Addiction record to his brief flirtation with the Red Hot Chili Peppers and on to a solo career—and back again—Navarro is the one guitarist who has been able to force the alternative and mainstream rock guitar worlds together and make it work every time.

As a member of incredibly high-profile alternative hard rock bands, Navarro can rightfully be credited with taking hard rock out of the mainstream and steering it down some of music's most intriguing side streets. An uncompromising musician, he has always managed to come up with the unique and unexpected, regardless of what band or genre he finds himself in.

BIOGRAPHY

Born on June 7, 1967, in Los Angeles, Dave Navarro played piano in grade school but gave it up after a few years. It wasn't until he heard Jimi Hendrix songs blasting over the PA at a local skateboard hangout that he decided he wanted to play guitar. And it wasn't about style or technical ability—Navarro wanted to play guitar that sounded and felt as psychedelic and loud as Hendrix's.

His father bought him an acoustic when he was 11, and his cousin Dan (currently of the acoustic guitar duo Lowen & Navarro) taught him some basic chords. When it came to song appreciation, though, his earliest guitar influences were at opposite ends of the spectrum: classic hard rockers Clapton, Hendrix, and Page on one side, and early British alt-rockers like the Cure's Robert Smith and Love and Rockets' Daniel Ash at the other.

His first band played covers of classics by Cream and Zeppelin. His other public music performances were in the marching band at Notre Dame high school—as a drummer. There he met fellow drummer Stephen Perkins, whose interest in music was similarly influenced by classic hard rock. The two formed a speed-metal band that played in and around Los Angeles. Along the way, they met bassist Eric Avery, whose sister had dated both Navarro and Perkins. Avery was in a band called Jane's Addiction, fronted by vocalist/artist Perry Farrell. Avery and Farrell invited Perkins to be their drummer, then decided they needed a new guitarist as well. Navarro became the fourth member of Jane's Addiction.

Navarro brought a twisted hard rock approach to Jane's avant-punk musicality, fusing a heavily distorted and psychedelic guitar style with Farrell's visceral glam vocals. The band was soon a staple on Hollywood's Sunset Strip, yet its metal-glam-punk-goth style was an anomaly amongst the big-hair bands that were the mainstays of L.A.'s club scene. Part of Jane's appeal was its image as glam-outfitted, hell-bent-for-self-destruction post-punks. Sex, drugs, and rock 'n' roll, sutured together with a generous nod to perversion, fashioned Jane's as a band living and teetering on the edge.

Jane's Addiction released its self-titled debut on Triple X Records in 1987, at the height of the shred metal era. Although under-produced and remarkably raw, the album proved that Jane's was like nothing else in Hollywood or anywhere else. More important, it showcased Navarro as a unique and wildly innovative guitarist who played against the grain of in-vogue shred metallers. The album started a bidding war by major labels that resulted in a deal with Warner Bros.

The first record for Warner Bros., 1988's *Nothing's Shocking*, was a sonic blast of everything that Navarro had learned and absorbed in the previous decade. It was a mix of metal, psychedelia, alternative, goth, and even punk, all woven in and around Farrell's tormented coyote howling. From the experimental guitar of "Ted, Just Admit It" to the atmospheric "Summertime Rolls," Navarro slipped easily in and out of unrelated rock styles that ranged from metal to dreampop, delivering it with a textured and dense sound that—while filling up all available tape space—never felt forced or busy.

Jane's followed up with 1990's *Ritual de lo Habitual.* Although not as groundbreaking as its predecessor, *Ritual* was a crossover success that gained the band mainstream acceptance—which probably ran counter to what they were hoping for. The group began to implode from its own success and chemical excess, both of which helped fuel an increased loathing between Farrell and Navarro. Opting out of the mainstream, Farrell decided to pull Jane's plug, taking the band out on the first Lollapalooza tour as their swansong. When Jane's finally flatlined, Navarro briefly considered leaving the record industry and opening a bookstore. Instead, he took Avery and formed the band Deconstruction. It was a short-lived project, lasting just long enough to produce one overlooked album.

Skirting back around the fringes of L.A.—and battling a drug habit he'd been working on since he was 15, when his mother was killed by her ex-boyfriend— Navarro was reportedly offered the guitar slot in Guns N' Roses. But he turned it down, choosing to join the Red Hot Chili Peppers instead. The pairing was ironic:

CHECKLIST ✓

Guitars . . . . Fender Custom Shop Strat, Parker Fly, PRS

Setup . . . . Standard

Strings . . . . Dean Markley .009–.042

Pickups . . . . Stock

Amplification . . . Marshall JCM900 4100, Marshall Mode Four MF350, 4x12 cabinets

Effects . . . . Lots of them, used regularly: Boss DD-3 Digital Delay, Boss DS-2 Turbo Distortion, Crybaby wah, EBow sustainer, Heil Talk Box, Dunlop Rotovibe

Tone . . . . From thick and syrupy to sharp and stinging

Attack . . . . Just hard enough to get the message across

Signature traits . . . . Drones, experimental sounds, atmospheric chords

Influences . . . . . . Jimi Hendrix, Daniel Ash, Robert Smith

Overall approach . . . . Get a wicked sound, and then go with the feel

SELECTED DISCOGRAPHY

Solo albums
Trust No One (Capitol, 2001)

With Jane's Addiction
Jane's Addiction (Triple X, 1987)
Nothing's Shocking (Warner Bros.,1988)
Ritual de lo Habitual (Warner Bros.,1990)
Strays (Capitol, 2003)

With Deconstruction
Deconstruction (Warner Bros., 1994)

With the Red Hot Chili Peppers
One Hot Minute (Warner Bros., 1995)

RECOMMENDED CUTS
"Jane Says" (*Jane's Addiction*)
"Stop" (*Ritual de lo Habitual*)
"Warped" (*One Hot Minute*)
"One Big Mob" (*One Hot Minute*)
"Rexall" (*Trust No One*)
"Had a Dad" (*Nothing's Shocking*)
"Just Because" (*Strays*)
"Strays" (*Strays*)
"To Match the Sun" (*Strays*)

Navarro was a relative newcomer to the music world compared to the Peppers, but it was the success of Jane's that brought bands like the Peppers the kind of mainstream attention they'd been seeking for years. With Navarro on board, the Peppers were as dysfunctional and chemically dependent as they'd ever been, and an album was a long time in coming.

When *One Hot Minute* was released in 1995, it proved to be substantially different from anything the band had ever done. Navarro's swirling guitar work, especially on songs like "Warped," filled out the Peppers' typically sparse funk arrangements. Notably, his playing forced vocalist Anthony Keidis to stay in key, something that longtime Peppers fans weren't used to. Usually the singer could waltz atonally around the minimalist guitar playing that had defined the band, but Navarro's approach required a more musical commitment.

Ultimately, the relationship didn't work out, perhaps because Navarro's playing was too layered and intense for the Peppers and their fans. He bowed out of the band with little fanfare and no apparent acrimony (former Pepper guitarist John Frusciante, who was the polar opposite of Navarro in everything from taste to style, was invited back in).

Interestingly, Navarro found himself on call for session work, his unusual approach to all forms of music making him a unique addition to recordings in a variety of genres. He appeared on albums from acts as diverse as Nine Inch Nails, Alanis Morrisette, Christina Aguilera, Michelle Branch, and Lowen & Navarro. In 2001 he released *Trust No One*, a solo album he had been working on since leaving the Peppers. Featuring the single "Rexall," it introduced Navarro to listeners not only as a talented guitarist but also as a lead vocalist.

His solo career didn't last long, although not for lack of interest. In 2003 he and Perry Farrell buried the hatchet and put Jane's back together, producing the excellent *Strays*. The album picked up where *Ritual* left off, replete with hallucinogenic multitracked guitars drenching every track. The success of *Strays* and its snarling amphetamine-guitar single "Just Because" led to the first Jane's tour in more than a decade.

Navarro's stock went up as well. His private life became public fodder when he and ubiquitous pin-up babe Carmen Electra had their courtship and wedding served up via the MTV reality show *'Til Death Do Us Part*. The show's title recalled not only a wedding vow but was also a wink to Navarro's fascination with death and darkness. For a guy so fascinated with the dark side, Navarro seems to bask in the bright glow of the spotlight, even appearing on TV to play celebrity poker. He's also spending time in his "glorified cover band," known as Camp Freddy.

No one is quite sure what Navarro's next role will be (other than that of Carmen Electra's bedmate), although it certainly seems as if he is at a point where he could pick and choose his next project. His constant evolution—as opposed to reinvention—has made his guitar work worth listening to every time he lays down a track. Wherever he ends up, he'll be doing something that no other hard rock guitarist is doing. It'll be bizarre, it'll be off-kilter, it'll be nasty and menacing, and it'll be some of the best rock guitar out there.

GEAR & SETUP

For all his otherworldly sounds, Navarro's basic setup is straightforward. He used Paul Reed Smith guitars for much of his early Jane's Addiction playing, and then he switched to Fender Custom Shop Stratocasters when he joined the Peppers—professing that the Strat was lighter-sounding and more suited to the trebly funkiness of the Peppers' material. On tour with the Peppers, he used a Parker Fly Classic. Navarro has stated he chose that guitar for its light weight, claiming his hands and body are too small for heavier and thicker guitars.

That said, he admits that he has relied a number of different guitars and will pick among nearly two dozen guitars and half a dozen amps to get the sounds he's looking for. His guitars have included Gibson Les Pauls, Flying V's, and SGs; Danelectros; and a variety of others. When composing, he chooses a guitar that has the right feel for what he wants to play, and he will work on the amp and effects setup later to get the tone close to what he wants to hear. But it starts with the guitar—if it doesn't feel right, the tune doesn't proceed.

In deference to his idol, Jimi Hendrix, Navarro's amps have typically been Marshalls, primarily a JCM900 4100 head through 4x12 cabs (notably a 1960BV straight cab). For dirty sounds, he uses old Marshalls; for clean sound, he uses newer Marshalls, typically running through the lead channel. He has also used a Marshall

Mode Four MF350 head for his clean tone. He also uses Bogner heads in the studio, and he has used an old Silvertone amp. He cranks his amps to the highest level of gain possible.

Navarro claims to be using many of the same effect pedals he had as a kid, and some of his devices are almost antique by modern standards. These include an EBow sustainer ("One Big Mob"), a Heil Talk Box, a Boss DD-3 Digital Delay, a Boss DS-2 Turbo Distortion, a Dunlop Rotovibe, and an original Vox Crybaby wah. Unlike most of his hard rock contemporaries, Navarro employs his effects liberally when recording, often piling one on top of another. With the amount of multitracking that he does, it's easy to lose track of where one guitar leaves off and the next one begins.

Because of his approach to recording—he fills up available space as much as possible—Navarro knows it's impossible to recreate everything onstage. As such, he tends to wing it and play the parts that he feels come across best live and that fill the most gaps. Onstage he has a very simple setup: two JCM900s going through two 4x12 straight and two slant cabinets. His live effects are a Dunlop Crybaby and a raft of Boss pedals, including chorus, digital delay, phase, and the Turbo Distortion.

Navarro uses Dean Markley strings gauged .009–.042. He plays with a pick and not his fingers. Despite the otherworldly sounds he gets on record—both from drones and from unusual note choices—the only alternate tuning he employs is dropped *D*.

STYLE & TECHNIQUE

Though at first listen Navarro's technique appears to be all over the map, he actually has a firm grip on all his influences and directs them with a laser-like focus. The one constant is that he doesn't allow for a lot of dead air. Even when the music is light and slow, his guitar is still churning away. He'll even use an acoustic under his electrics to provide another textural bed.

His rhythm guitars are used not only for propelling a beat (his bands have traditionally had excellent drummers), but also for creating droning atmospherics that are mixed way off in the distance. Layers upon layers of rhythms and even single notes are built into ethereal, quasi-psychedelic sounds that weave in and out of the main themes. His playing works its way up the neck, and he's not afraid to forgo the typical low-end barre chords of hard rock in favor of stinging, trebly partial chords and double-stops.

Meanwhile, his solos are based on classic rock but are replete with squonky squeals in the vein of experimentalists from Hendrix and Fripp to Belew and Vai. Navarro is a restless player—especially when approaching the resolution of a phrase, when he'll scoop, bend, or otherwise put that expected tone through the grinder. Likewise, a solo entrance may begin in a pentatonic position, as so many solos in standard rock do, but he'll deliver his ideas with blissfully grating whammy-bar tremolo to yank the notes off pitch. He loves to kick in the wah pedal for his solos, not just for its high- and low-end filtering but to leave it halfway depressed for an out-of-phase sound.

As noted above, the feel comes first, followed by the tone. He cites Jeff Beck's playing as an influence in this regard. Navarro doesn't read music, and he tends to feel his way around the neck to come up with the right pattern or progression. In fact, many of his riff-like pieces are actually quickly shuffled chords.

Navarro admits to filling up every unused track available to him in the studio. If he's recording with a band and he has 15 tracks at his disposal, he'll use them all. His mantra is to leave no space unfilled.

Navarro is not too concerned about playing the "right" notes. He claims that Perry Farrell's eclectic approach to music taught him to think outside of blues boxes and scales, and if he hits a wrong note, he'll play it again to make it sound like it belongs.

LESSON

Rhythm parts like **Ex. 1**'s manage to imply groove and movement with relatively little effort. It all revolves around a simple *A5* chord and benefits from changing up the rhythms and register of surrounding notes. The groove comes by keeping your picking hand swinging so that every eighth-note is a downstroke and every 16th in between is an upstroke.

Track
12

Ex. 1

Here's a Navarro-like lead played over the rhythm part heard in Ex. 1. You'll need a trem bar to get the quivering vibrato on the opening double-stop—first bend with your left hand, then yank the double-stop up and shake the life out of it. Two "talking" wham-bar bends allow for a position transition that lands you in place for the full measure of hammer-and-pull on the 4th string. A bluesy descent follows, but don't land on the tonic *A*—get back up to the 6th-string *C* and give it a little bend.

Ex. 2

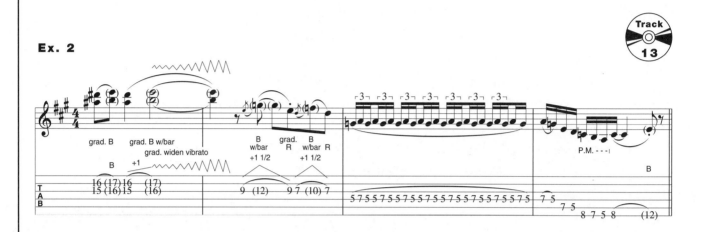

Example 3 requires a little cooperation between hands and feet. Rock a wah-wah pedal as you hammer from open 5th and 4th strings to frets 5 and 7. When the power chord hits, stomp on the pedal to turn it off. A measure later the wah is back on—pulled upward at first to dial back the high end, then gradually coming down as the note you're playing is bent up. Stomp again to turn it off and hit the power chord again, followed this time by octave fills.

A little bit of digital delay adds size and depth. When it all comes together, you'll get a part that mixes classic rock sensibility and newer, nastier elements.

Ex. 3

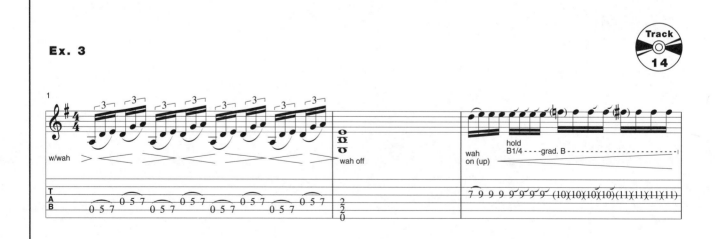

Navarro can deliver a razor-sharp lead on demand, and the wah pedal often helps him put an edge on it. Pick and pull angrily—but in control—for the first two bars of **Ex. 4** with the wah pedal on and holding steady about a quarter of the way off the floor. Then get it up fully for that slowly-throwing-up sound over the bent *C* (2nd string, 13th fret).

Notice how the middle four bars, which sound elastic and elongated, are sandwiched between rapid and frenetic parts. Altering your phrasing as Navarro does keeps the solo colorful and dynamic.

Ex. 4

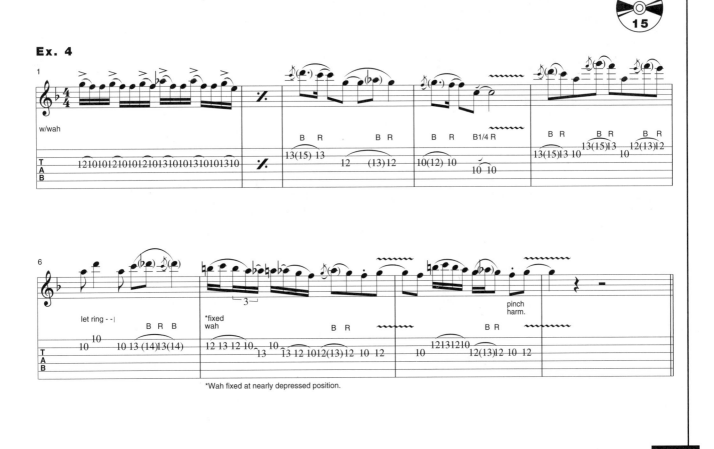

*Wah fixed at nearly depressed position.

In both Jane's Addiction and the Peppers, Navarro was called on to be a rhythmic home base for tunes that ventured into funk territory. One part Stevie Ray Vaughan and one part James Brown, **Ex. 5** features a Navarro approach as served up on a Strat. Stay aggressive, articulate every note, and stay dead on time; it may seem ironic, but a lot of funk parts get their feel by playing in very strict time.

Ex. 5

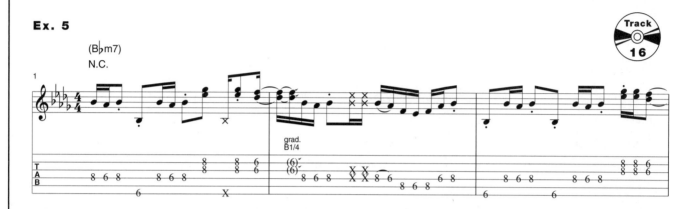

CHAPTER 5
Kim Thayil of Soundgarden

Soundgarden may have been the most successful and innovative hard rock band at the end of the 20th century. Mistakenly labeled as members of the grunge world, Soundgarden owed more to punk, psychedelia, and metal than any of its contemporaries did. Driven by the trippy and thundering guitar playing of Kim Thayil, Soundgarden kept the spirit of hard rock alive as the millennium approached, incorporating the innovation and experimentation of hard rock predecessors ranging from Zeppelin and Sabbath to Hendrix and Zappa.

In a band of exceptional musicians, Thayil was perhaps the most extreme, creating guitar parts that went the opposite direction of where they were expected to go, or playing riffs in time signatures that most hard rockers had never heard of, let alone could keep up with.

BIOGRAPHY

Kim Thayil was born on September 4, 1960, in Seattle, Washington, and grew up in Park Forest, a suburb of Chicago. His parents were from East India; his mother was a music teacher who had a degree from the Royal Academy of Music in London, and his father was an engineer. Kim's interest in the guitar came from wanting to write his own songs and play the things he heard on the radio. As a high school student, he locked himself away in his room with a Sears acoustic guitar for hours on end, figuring out chords by noodling around the fretboard. He absorbed and adapted just about everything he heard, creating a diverse palette from which he would later draw: Kiss, the New York Dolls, Television, Killing Joke, Frank Zappa, Jeff Beck, Jimi Hendrix, the Stooges, the Ramones, Bob Mould and Hüsker Dü, the Melvins, the Butthole Surfers, and even early Chicago were all influences.

In high school, he and bassist Hiro Yamamoto formed a rock band that they named after the cartoon character Zippy the Pinhead. After graduating from high school, Thayil, along with friends Yamamoto and Bruce Pavitt, headed west to Olympia, Washington, to attend Evergreen State College. In Washington, Pavitt started a fanzine called *Subterranean Pop*, which evolved into Sub Pop Records, while Thayil and Yamamoto played in various bands in and around Seattle. Yamamoto's roommate was drummer and vocalist Chris Cornell, and eventually Thayil, Cornell, and Yamamoto formed Soundgarden (named after a Seattle sculpture), later adding Matt Cameron on drums.

They signed to Pavitt's Sub Pop label in 1987 and released two EPs, *Screaming Life* and *FOPP*. Featuring heavy, metallic guitar coupled with Cornell's shrieking vocals, the records gained the band a following in the Pacific Northwest. Looking for bigger record distribution, Soundgarden hooked up with the indie-punk SST record label the following year, putting out *Ultramega OK*. That record's unique and harsh sound got the major labels interested, and the band signed with A&M, releasing *Louder Than Love* in 1990. Even though the arty post-punk ethic and fury of Soundgarden's recordings and performances defied easy definition, the band was summarily lumped into the alternative and hard rock category, based primarily on Cornell's decibel-defying vocals and Thayil's pummeling riffs, exemplified by cuts like "Loud Love" and "Big Dumb Sex."

Yamamoto left the band to return to school and was replaced by Ben Shepherd. With this solid lineup, Soundgarden was poised to be—and described as—the next big thing in rock music when it released *Badmotorfinger* in 1991. A barely describable album with incredibly catchy riffs, intelligent lyrics, and a dizzyingly hypnotic sound—epitomized by songs such as "Rusty Cage," "Face Pollution," and "Room a Thousand Years Wide"—*Badmotorfinger* had all the earmarks of a breakthrough.

The band toured in support of the record (and was even paired with Guns N' Roses), but suddenly found itself up against unexpected competition for the airwaves: Nirvana. The appearance of Cobain and company changed the musical landscape of the early 1990s, and *Nevermind* took the spot that many believed was due *Badmotorfinger*. Grunge and Seattle became the two buzzwords of the lemming-like music business, and Seattle bands of all stripes were signed to major labels as fast as the contracts could be drafted. The fact that Soundgarden had actually been ahead of this wave fixed them dead center in the media's focus, and they were thus tagged as grunge rockers.

Although the label was unfair, it certainly garnered the band a huge amount of attention. Yet Thayil, like Alice in Chains' Jerry Cantrell, was a much more musical and accomplished guitarist than any of the notable grunge players. His ability to riff and solo against the grain owed more to a class of musicians like Zappa and Jeff Beck than to the tossed-off rhythms of most grunge guitarists. Thayil and Soundgarden could play fast and they could play dirges; they could play dark and low in dropped *D*, bright and sparkly in open tunings, or completely off axis in tunings seldom heard outside of Sonic Youth (*EEBBBB, EEEEEE*—that's a tuning, not a scream). They could play in 9/8 just as easily as they played in 4/4, and make one as listenable and interesting as the other. Fusing these abilities produced a brand of psychedelic hard rock that was like a freeway collision between Black Sabbath and the Beatles. And the band made it work on every cylinder when they recorded *Superunknown.*

CHECKLIST ✓

Guitar . . . . Guild S-100

Setup . . . . Standard

Strings . . . . Ernie Ball Super Slinkys, .009–.042

Pickups . . . . Humbuckers

Amplification . . . Mesa/Boogie Dual Rectifiers, 50-watt Mavericks

Settings . . . . Low end on full, midrange at 11 o'clock, treble at 2 o'clock

Effects . . . . Dunlop Crybaby wah

Tone . . . . Sludgy yet sharp

Attack . . . . Heavy when necessary, light as called for

Signature traits . . . . Off-kilter time signatures, droning

Influences . . . . . . Ace Frehley, Jimi Hendrix, Jeff Beck, Paul Leary, Frank Zappa

Overall approach . . . . Loud and ferocious, with textured overtones and layers

SELECTED DISCOGRAPHY

Ultramega OK (SST, 1989)
Louder Than Love (A&M, 1990)
Badmotorfinger (A&M, 1991)
Superunknown (A&M, 1994)
Down on the Upside (A&M, 1996)
Probot (Southern Lord, 2004)

RECOMMENDED CUTS

"Loud Love" (*Louder Than Love*)
"Big Dumb Sex" (*Louder Than Love*)
"Rusty Cage" (*Badmotorfinger*)
"Jesus Christ Pose" (*Badmotorfinger*)
"Room a Thousand Years Wide"
   (*Badmotorfinger*)
"My Wave" (*Superunknown*)
"Superunknown" (*Superunknown*)
"Pretty Noose" (*Down on the Upside*)
"Never the Machine Forever" (*Down on the Upside*)

Superunknown was Soundgarden's long-delayed breakout. While everyone was tossing it into the grunge net, Soundgarden had expanded and matured to the point where it could no longer be pigeonholed with any other band. Thayil, in particular, combined the best of modern guitar styles with his well-traveled '70s roots and brought his inimitable sound to full maturity. It was as far from grunge as it was from heavy metal, yet it owed plenty to both genres, as well as to punk and psychedelia. From the howling unisons on "My Wave" to the molasses drudge of "4th of July," his playing on *Superunknown* was all over the map—in the best sense of the phrase. The record produced some certified radio staples, including "Spoonman" and "Black Hole Sun," and it brought Soundgarden the kind of fame everyone believed the band had always deserved.

Success did not come without a price, however. Everyone in Soundgarden wrote songs, and most of them could play guitar. While Thayil had been the primary songwriter on early records, Cornell and Shepherd were now contributing the lion's share of the tunes. Plus, Cornell was playing more and more of his own guitar parts live and on record. When the follow-up to *Superunknown, Down on the Upside*, came out in 1996, Thayil contributed only one composition ("Never the Machine Forever"), while some of the lead guitar was actually performed by Cornell. Yet *Down on the Upside* was a stellar record, perhaps the ultimate synthesis of everything that Thayil brought to the band. It was fast, slow, thick, thin, bright, dark, jagged, smooth, and vicious—and that was just on the cut "Pretty Noose."

It was evident that Soundgarden was increasingly following Cornell's direction and not Thayil's, although there was never a public rift. A year later, the band announced that it was folding. No big blowup, no drugged-out members checking into rehab. They were just done.

While Cornell soon hooked up with Rage Against the Machine's Tom Morello to form Audioslave, Thayil has been content to remain out of the spotlight. He has occasionally shown up as lead guitarist on under-the-radar projects like Dave Grohl's *Probot* record in 2004 and as a guest in drummer Matt Cameron's band, Wellwater Conspiracy.

Despite Soundgarden's implosion, Thayil had reached a point in his playing where he could effortlessly meld the best styles of his forebears and not make them sound like they were just tossed into a musical blender. In the hands of a lesser guitarist, albums like *Superunknown* and *Badmotorfinger* might have sounded like a play-by-numbers version of the best that early hard rock guitarists had to offer. As it turned out, Thayil's off-kilter approach to combining all of his influences made Soundgarden as unique as any band that has recorded in the last two decades.

Ultimately, Thayil is worth listening to for his ability to weave Soundgarden's songs from the real roots of heavy rock. Not a bluesman, not a metal monger, not a grungemeister, Kim Thayil managed to be the perfect synthesis of all those worlds while adding an exoticism that is his alone.

GEAR & SETUP

Thayil's gear is as diverse as his influences and his styles. He is most frequently associated with a white Guild S-100—which looks like a Gibson SG—although that guitar gave up the ghost when he threw it into his amp during a show. He has used other S-100s but has never limited himself to that instrument. On *Superunknown*, he used a '59 Fender Telecaster for songs with dropped tunings. The Tele's fixed tailpiece was best for the alt tunings, and its emphasis of the upper midrange helped create more room for the bass on that album. Thayil has said his "discovery" of the Tele during those sessions gave him a taste for single-coils for the first time and even influenced his writing. He has also used Gibson Les Pauls, Fender Jazzmasters, and Epiphones.

Thayil varies his guitar settings wildly within songs and solos. Always one to flip a finger at convention, Thayil would often utilize the bridge pickup for rhythm playing and the neck pickup for lead. The roundness of the neck pickup made for some surprisingly "soft" tones in very aggressive solos, and by combining its roundness with boosted treble controls he could produce a sound that was both full and bright.

In the studio, Thayil has used Mesa/Boogie Dual Rectifiers for solos while employing Mesa 50-watt Mavericks for rhythm tracks. With the Rectifiers, he used the tube setting for a warm sound (something he calls "mellow brightness"). He also has used a 65-watt Music Man head running through 4x12 cabinets, as well as a

Fender Super Reverb, a Fender Princeton, a Fender Twin Reverb, and even an Orange head. On most of his amps, the low end is cranked way up, the midrange is set to 11 o'clock, and the treble is set to 2 o'clock.

Thayil has occasionally used outboard preamps, notably the Intellitronics LA-2 and the Summit, for recording with a direct input.

Like many hard rock guitarists, Thayil is not a big user of effects, a fact that may reflect his early punk influence. However, he has relied heavily on one pedal: a Dunlop Crybaby wah (and occasionally a ColorSound wah). He likes to leave the wah on when it's in his signal chain so it can sharpen some tones and augment some of his droning noise. He also used it to help his leads cut through the often sludge-like tone of the entire band, as well as to accent individual note bends. Other effects, always used sparingly, have included a Rotovibe (in the Rotovibe setting, not the chorus), Ibanez stereo chorus pedal, and a Mu-Tron phase shifter.

Thayil uses Ernie Ball Super Slinkys (.009–.042), but for dropped tunings, he switches to heavy-bottom/light-top gauges. His picks are Dunlop .73s, although he's gone as thin as .60 and as heavy as .88. He holds the pick like a small club, gripping it with thumb, first, and middle fingers, and then rotates it over the strings for speed. For rhythm attack, he's very much a proponent of the Ramones' style of downpicking, or repeated downstroking.

STYLE & TECHNIQUE

Thayil's playing can be angry, chaotic, and melodic, often in the same song. Some of this is tonal, some is time-related, some is an extension of the songwriting, but mostly it's Thayil's left-of-center approach to the guitar. He often solos in alternate tunings, which makes for some weird note choices. ("That doesn't make it easy," he once said, "but then again, it opens you up to different sounds.") Even in standard tuning, he rarely resolves phrases in expected places. And though his riffing has shades of Black Sabbath running through it, he manages to turn 180 degrees in the middle of a progression and go from dirge-like hammering to airy pop lines.

Beyond the exotic scales and harmonies, Thayil's style incorporates a great deal of noise, and he always seems to be torturing his guitar into some new timbre. In quieter moments, he has alchemized some truly grating tones into something gorgeous. It was also characteristic for him to juxtapose very rapid lead passages against Soundgarden's slowest rhythms.

Soundgarden played in a lot of odd time signatures, a reflection of the many songwriters in the band and the fact that Cornell used to be a drummer. From 7/4 to 9/8 to 13/8, Thayil had to be on top of the weird rhythms, which he said comes naturally to him in songwriting. Interestingly, he once reported he was more thrown by the 4/4 parts in Cornell's compositions when Cornell would place guitar parts on upbeats.

Thayil is known for his wide Tony Iommi–like vibrato—which he claims was inspired by Paul Leary of the Butthole Surfers—and the long, slow bends that characterize many drudging Soundgarden riffs. Instead of rocking his hand at the wrist, he usually pushes the string up and down vertically across the neck. This isn't as subtle as the wrist-rocking style, but it gets the point across. His vibrato has an alter ego, however, with many sustained solo notes treated to a frenetic shimmer. He also drones quite a bit, relying on feedback to get his strings to vibrate (primarily the dropped 6th string) and adding some layering to the overall sound.

Soundgarden was fond of alternative tunings, notably dropped *D* and (low to high) *CGCGGE*. Thayil likes doubling up strings with the same note to get a chorus effect or to create layered droning. It also gives him a chance to explore new chord possibilities. He plays his solos in the altered tuning, primarily for the convenience of not having to change guitars, but also because he feels it creates moments of serendipity when he's forced to think outside convenient fingerings to find the right notes.

In the studio, Cornell would play some of his own rhythm parts, and Thayil would either double the part or add fills and a solo. He doesn't write his solos down in advance, although he will create actual solo parts that he feels will complement instrumental passages. On those occasions when he's spontaneous, he'll improvise a solo and then go back, relearn the part, and double it or even overdub an octave up.

LESSON

Kim Thayil had a major love affair with punk, and the influences of the Stooges, MC5, and Johnny Ramone came out in Soundgarden's early days. For **Ex. 1**, concentrate less on getting all the strokes in as on nailing the beats. Check those hoedown hammers in bars 5 and 6—just get a half-step behind *G* on the 4th string, 4th fret, to double the open *G*. Note all the octaves and unisons in here, especially the brief double-*E* blast before the return to the octave *D*'s. Yeah.

Ex. 1

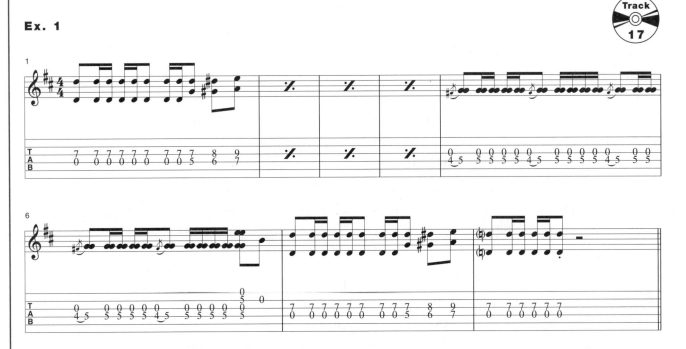

The thumping, lumbering riff in **Ex. 2** combines 5 chords and single notes in 7/4 time. Like the best tunes written outside of standard time signatures, this doesn't *feel* odd, and Kim has said he's comfortable with 7's and 9's. All the 5 chords are palm-muted, making the single notes really stand out. Note the early bend on low *F* (6th string, 3rd fret); by contrast, the *D* and *C* played alone on the 5th string sit out there bare-assed, with no finger vibrato or anything. *On the CD: Mind the long count-off for 7/4 time.*

Ex. 2

Thayil's leads are always a wild ride, and at least five different approaches inform the solo in **Ex. 3**. Though Thayil's ideas do seem to come from outer space—in part a result of comping disparate ideas into a single solo—his thoughts are organized in melodic phrases, often very different ones from measure to measure.

Characteristic moves include Thayil's rapid trills and overbends, and his avoiding the expected. He also likes to solo with a wah pedal on, even if it's in one position for much of the lead.

Ex. 3

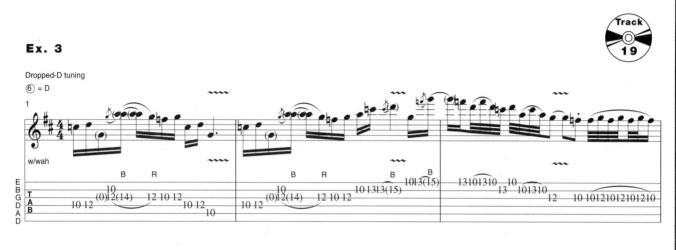

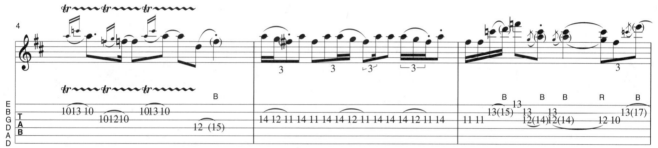

One element of Thayil's spacey parts is that he doesn't go overboard with effects. However much he may put his instrument through the ringer—with wah, amp vibrato, finger vibrato—it always sounds like a *guitar* (at least an electric one in the post-Hendrix world).

The approach for **Ex. 4** is definitely left of center, but in a part like this Thayil manages to play something ethereal while combining noise and a kind of softness. Use the wah sparingly, never taking it too far in either extreme.

Ex. 4

CHAPTER 6
Jerry Cantrell of Alice in Chains

Of all the hard rockers who emerged in the 1990s, Jerry Cantrell may have had the single biggest impact on the current state of hard rock. As an extremely accomplished player, he's certainly been the most emulated. The sound he created for Alice in Chains—dark, ominous, brutal, and melodic, all at the same time—demonstrated that Cantrell was more thoughtful about his playing than most of the grunge guitarists who appeared at the same time.

The tone of his guitar is one of the deepest, and most menacing, found on records in any genre. Yet he offsets his guitar's metallic snarling by creating melodic structure rarely found in metal or grunge—perfect for hard rock with attitude. His ability to rein in disparate styles and emotions makes him a player of enormous taste and restraint—even if his music's threatening guise makes it sound like all bets are off.

BIOGRAPHY

Jerry Cantrell was born in Tacoma, Washington, on March 18, 1966. He was 14 years old and a member of the high school choir when he got his first guitar, though it resided in his closet for a few years before he got the itch to play it. By the time he picked it up, the instrument had only two strings, but that didn't stop Cantrell from working out riffs by heavy rockers AC/DC and Kiss, his two acknowledged biggest influences.

While taking his guitar cues from hard rockers and metal heads, Cantrell's writing was influenced by '70s-era popsters from Elton John to Fleetwood Mac as well as by country-and-western artists like Willie Nelson and Merle Haggard. The melodies these musicians created would infuse Cantrell's playing style. Even with a bottom-heavy and metallic guitar sound, his riffs and chord progressions were fluid and melodic.

In 1987 Cantrell hooked up with the musicians who would later form Alice in Chains: vocalist Layne Staley, bassist Mike Starr, and drummer Sean Kinney. The band created heavy songs—written primarily by Cantrell—with layered vocal harmonies (Staley and Cantrell's) that established the group as more progressive musically than other bands in the burgeoning Seattle grunge scene.

Alice in Chains signed to Columbia Records in 1989 and released its first LP, *Facelift*, the following year. The record was extraordinarily dark and heavy, building on Cantrell's catchy riffs and Staley's tortured vocals. The first singles, "We Die Young" and "Man in the Box," were indicative of the band's sound but not of its range. Many of the album's cuts featured lugubrious riffing *à la* Black Sabbath, with flourishes of '70s-era soloing. For lack of an appropriate description, and because the band was from Seattle, Alice in Chains was classified by some as metal slamming head-on into grunge—although the record took off via its heavy rotation on metal radio stations.

As if to shed both the metal and the grunge tags, AIC followed *Facelift* with an all-acoustic EP, *Sap*. Instead of being grunge unplugged, it was a showcase for Cantrell's intricate and interesting playing style, which recalled some of the quieter moments of English prog bands like Jethro Tull. The record also featured string arrangements, which further removed the band from easy categorization.

The next record, 1992's *Dirt*, came to be the definitive Alice in Chains album. Cantrell served up an entire range of hard rock offerings, from the swirling nightmare haze of "Would?" to the heavy riff of "Rooster." His influences, from Jimmy Page, Ace Frehley, Brian May, David Gilmour, and Robin Trower to Tony Iommi, Davey Johnstone, and Lindsey Buckingham, were evident across the album's tunes, which were densely layered and unlike anything else available at the time. In fact,

AIC may have been the only band in America selling unadulterated hard rock for its own sake in the early 1990s.

The band went on tour with Van Halen (and new bassist Mike Inez) following the release of *Dirt*. Between shows, Cantrell and Eddie Van Halen struck up a friendship, with Van Halen giving Cantrell some of his signature equipment, including an Ernie Ball guitar that would later become a staple of Cantrell's setup.

In the aftermath of *Dirt*, Staley's drug problem knocked the band off its feet, forcing it to bail out of several major festival appearances and tour dates. Nonetheless, AIC released a second EP, 1994's *Jar of Flies*, a record that found the band exploring both the lightest and heaviest elements of its sound. Featuring deft electric and acoustic guitar from Cantrell, the album's range of styles recalled the light heaviness of *Physical Graffiti*–era Led Zeppelin, a factor that helped the album find its way into the collections of more fans.

The band returned in 1995 with *Alice in Chains*, its third and last full-length studio record. The album was dark and painful even by AIC standards, stuffed to overflowing with dirge-like Cantrell offerings such as "Grind" and "Sludge Factory." Although well produced and musically diverse, there were few bright spots to slice through the oppressive gloom.

The band went on extended hiatus while Staley tried to straighten himself out, his drug addiction an obvious source of problems and no longer just speculation. Cantrell recorded some solo soundtrack and tribute album tunes, notably for *The*

CHECKLIST ✓

Guitars . . . . G&L Rampage and ASAT,
Gibson Les Pauls,
Ernie Ball EVH

Setup . . . . Standard

Strings . . . . Dean Markley, .009–.046

Pickups . . . . Seymour Duncan Jeff Beck

Amplification . . . Bogner, Mesa/Boogie Dual
Rectifiers, Peavey 5150,
Marshall 4x12 cabinets

Effects . . . . Dunlop Crybaby wah

Tone . . . . Aggressive and menacing

Attack . . . . Heavy but laid-back, with
the force coming from the
amp rather than aggressive
picking

**Signature
traits** . . . . Meaty power chords,
languid solos

Influences . . . . . Ace Frehley, Brian May,
Tony Iommi

**Overall
approach** . . . . Punishing tone and riffs,
but knows exactly when to
back off

SELECTED DISCOGRAPHY

With Alice in Chains
Facelift (Columbia, 1990)
Sap EP (Columbia, 1992)
Dirt (Columbia, 1992)
Jar of Flies EP (Columbia, 1994)
Alice in Chains (Columbia, 1995)
Solo albums
Unplugged (Columbia, 1996)
Boggy Depot (Columbia, 1998)
Degradation Trip (Roadrunner, 2002)

RECOMMENDED CUTS

"Man in the Box" (*Facelift*)
"Put You Down" (*Facelift*)
"Dam That River" (*Dirt*)
"I Stay Away" (*Jar of Flies*)
"No Excuses" (*Jar of Flies*)
"Grind" (*Alice in Chains*)
"So Close" (*Alice in Chains*)
"Anger Rising" (*Degradation Trip*)
"Dickeye" (*Boggy Depot*)

Cable Guy and *Twisted Willie*. Alice in Chains pulled itself together briefly for an episode of MTV's *Unplugged* (with second guitarist Scott Olson), recorded at the Brooklyn Academy of Music in 1996. It would be the band's last official recording, and it became one of the most successful of MTV's myriad *Unplugged* releases. Then Alice in Chains disappeared—but never officially broke up.

While everyone waited for Staley to take a vacation from his syringe and smack, Cantrell recorded his first solo album, 1998's *Boggy Depot*. The record revealed him to be the brains, heart, and soul of AIC, from guitars to vocals to arrangements—*Boggy Depot* could easily have passed for an AIC album. Cantrell toured behind the record, taking along second guitarist Chris DeGarmo, who had recently quit his own band, Queensrÿche.

With still no word from the AIC camp, Cantrell followed up two years later with *Degradation Trip*, an album as haunting as anything Alice in Chains had ever done. Its first single, "Anger Rising," encapsulated Cantrell in a single song: a menacing, even leering, riff that sounded like an angry machine (offset with some acoustic guitar), stellar harmonies, pained childhood memories, and a head-snapping chorus. *Degradation Trip* was released in two parts during 2002, allowing Cantrell to put out the album the record company wanted as well as the one he wanted.

All the while, he held the door open for an Alice in Chains reunion, but it would never happen. As *Degradation Trip* was about to be released, Layne Staley died from a heroin overdose—he'd been dead in his apartment for two weeks before anyone found him. The coroner ruled that Staley's death had occurred on April 5, 2002, eight years to the day from the date that Kurt Cobain killed himself.

After a brief period out of the spotlight, Cantrell re-emerged in 2004, appearing at a number of charity events and one-off appearances. He and Cult guitarist Billy Duffy announced that they were forming a jam band, an idea that appealed to Cantrell after appearing in Dave Navarro's Camp Freddy jam band.

Since Cantrell is still recording, we're sure to hear more from him, either as a solo artist or as a member of another band. Rock guitarists will certainly await the next release anxiously; Cantrell's influence in current rock is significant, perhaps more than any other modern hard rock guitarist. His shattered-concrete riffs and tone can be found in the band's numerous current-generation clones, the most obvious of which is Godsmack, which took not only its riffs and vocal style from AIC, but also its name—"God Smack" was a track on *Dirt*.

But Cantrell remains head and shoulders above his imitators. Whereas many hard rock guitarists of lesser stature have made their mark by pummeling their guitars—note the staccato fever of the late 1990s—Cantrell's sound came more from squeezing or throttling the sound out of his guitar. There was less mechanical brutality and more of a natural musical progression in Cantrell's approach to the instrument. In this way he's like Dave Navarro: He's a classic-rock revivalist, but rather than rehashing old riffs, he uses what was interesting then to explore new territory.

GEAR & SETUP

In the gear realm, as with his playing style, Jerry Cantrell puts to use a wide array of instruments. While his equipment choices have changed noticeably over the years, for most of his Alice in Chains work he used a G&L Rampage guitar. At the time, he claimed they were the most comfortable guitars he'd ever picked up. The Rampages were fitted to Jerry's standards, which included Seymour Duncan Jeff Beck pickups in the treble position and Kahler tremolo bars, mods he deployed to make the guitars as close as possible to a cross between a Les Paul and a Stratocaster. In addition to the Rampages, he played G&L ASAT guitars.

Eddie Van Halen gave him an Ernie Ball EVH signature model (made prior to Van Halen's jump to Peavey), which showed up on record and onstage. During his solo years, Cantrell appeared more frequently with Gibson Les Pauls, notably Les Paul Customs, Standards, and a Les Paul Junior he bought from Nancy Wilson of Heart. (Heart provided studio space and equipment to many Seattle bands during the '90s.) He occasionally uses Fender Stratocasters, including one from the early '60s. His notable acoustic guitars were borrowed from Nancy Wilson and bassist Mike Inez.

Which guitar Cantrell uses when is hard to pin down, as he and his guitar tech bring in anywhere from 40 to 50 different guitars to be toyed with in the studio. For Cantrell, it has to feel right in order for him to play it right.

His strings and picks are pretty much the stock-in-trade of most hard rock players—the strings are light Dean Markleys, .009–.046., while the picks are heavy Jim Dunlops.

For alternate tunings, Cantrell uses dropped *D*, as well as some open tunings that he makes up by playing with sounds in the studio. He often tunes down as far as 1½ steps, his love of the low further evidenced by occasional use of a baritone guitar.

Amplification is a massive part of Cantrell's sound. His early Alice in Chains amps were Bogners, including the Fish preamp and a Bogner Shiva head that was also used in his live solo performances. But Cantrell has experimented with some of the other classics of hard rock, notably Mesa Dual Rectifiers. Van Halen gave him some Peavey EVH 5150s, which Cantrell took into the studio because of their fatter and "wilder" tone. Other amps that have made an appearance include a Tube Works MosValve 500 power amp, some Soldanos and Marshalls, and a Fender Twin Reverb for his acoustics.

Effects are always noticeable in his tone—though its sheer ferocity tends to minimize the impact of effects—and Cantrell has quite a few. His favorite far and away is a Dunlop Crybaby wah, which is heard throughout his recorded work. He uses it at full throttle, getting a true sweep through the wah-wah spectrum for both riffs and leads. He also uses a Dunlop Rotovibc, an Electro-Harmonix Big Muff π distortion, a ProCo Rat, an Eventide Harmonizer, and a Maestro Phaser.

His live setup includes a variety of the above amp heads, usually played through eight 4x12 Marshall cabs with Celestion 30-watt speakers. The most consistent setup has been the Bogner Fish preamp driving the Mesa Simul-Class 2. His onstage rack effects include the addition of a BBE Sonic Maximizer and Rocktron RSP Intelliverb. He uses Nady and Samson wireless systems.

STYLE & TECHNIQUE

Jerry Cantrell's playing sounds like an undecorated and overheating locomotive. Much of it is about force—pulsing, vibrating, and ferocious. Stripped of frills and flash, his is an uncomplicated and brutish guitar style full of hammering chords and skull-pinching leads.

Cantrell's major achievement as a hard rock guitarist is that he melded the world of grunge (noisy, brash, emotional, and primitive) with the world of the metallist (ball-crushing tone, precision playing, and instrumental control).

His heavy, crunching tone accents an almost rootsy slow-blues style. His fills are reminiscent of the sounds of late-1960s arena solos: atmospheric and aggressive, but always to the point. They never crowd the song or the vocals. At times they even evoke major '60s and '70s player like Hendrix and Santana. There are few surprises in the direction of Jerry's solos, because they always fit naturally into the confines of the song. And unlike contemporaries Kim Thayil or Dave Navarro, Cantrell is willing to let empty space invade his playing, refusing to cram the instrument into every available opening.

Cantrell is also particular about where and when he applies his effects. For the most part, he relies on the strength of the tone from his guitar and amp setup. He does apply phase-shifting to his lighter electric and acoustic work, but he limits his effects to wah-wah and occasional reverb. The reverb is used primarily for his background fills, while the wah serves to add meat to his solos. The wah is also employed in order to provide a near-subliminal growl when he chooses to double a main riff into the guitar tracks. In all, his effects serve as mere shadows to the underlying guitar sound, and never actually drive his playing.

LESSON

Tune down one and a half steps to get the growl on for **Ex. 1**. The chromatics make for an especially sinister twist, and a little bend on the *E* (low string, 3rd fret) contributes that much more nastiness. The riff seems to turn over on itself, then comes to a dead stop before repeating. That's a move out of the metal guitar book: The volume seems greater in contrast to silence.

When tuned down this far, the strings can rattle on the neck, so pick closer to the bridge. But don't fight off the percussive sound of pick-on-pickups that Jerry seems to like so much. Our example was produced using compression and a DigiTech Whammy pedal.

Ex. 1

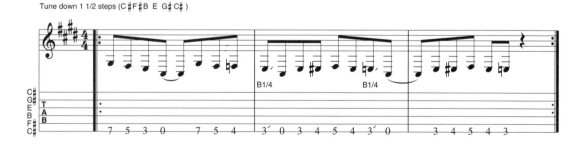

Cantrell has a way with rhythm-based hooks, as heard on tunes like "Rooster," "Would?," "Down in a Hole," and even the acoustic "No Excuses." By mixing chords and brief riffs—passing tones, really—he seems to evoke melodies from chord forms. **Example 2** is played on electric, with light distortion and light flanging.

Ex. 2

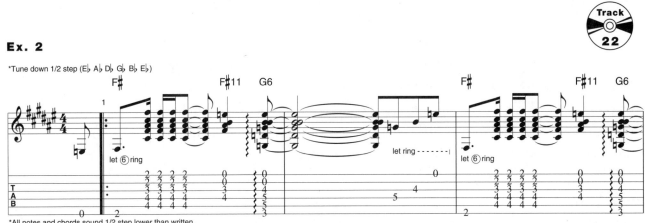

The acoustic in **Ex. 3** is arpeggiated, and the time is rock steady. While there are plenty of examples of rock tunes built on an acoustic bed, Cantrell makes even an arpeggio of steady eighths interesting. Primarily he accomplishes this by establishing a unique pattern. Though the entire four-measure part repeats exactly the same way the second time around, the note pattern is different within each measure. Plus, small variations—the absence of a bass note in the second measure, the pull-off in the fourth—keep a listener's ears piqued.

Ex. 3

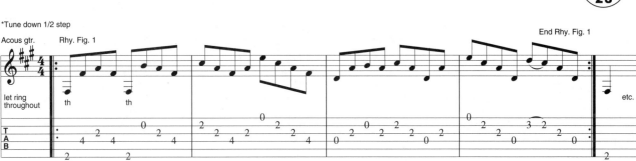

In **Ex. 4**, the previous acoustic arpeggio is heard beneath a "woman tone" lead. Humbucker guitars are great for getting that fat sound—just select the neck pickup and dial out the high end—but it's not hard to recreate the round, almost muffled tone on any guitar if you can roll back the treble and the high end of the midrange.

The lead here is patient, with lots of space and no rushed playing. Note how many beats it takes to get the first lead note up to pitch. The guitar goes into a harmony in the last few bars; Cantrell would often arrange guitars in harmonies similar to the lines he and Staley might sing.

All combined, the result is a guitar arrangement that falls somewhere between sad and haunted.

Ex. 4

Track
24

*Tune down 1/2 step
w/Rhy. Fig. 1 (Acous. gtr., 4 times)
Gtr. 2 (elec.)

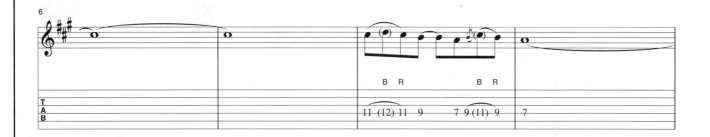

*All notes and chords sound 1/2 step lower than written.

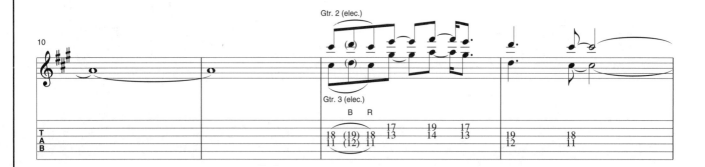

CHAPTER 7
Dean DeLeo of Stone Temple Pilots

When Dean DeLeo and Stone Temple Pilots hit the airwaves in the early 1990s, they were promptly dismissed as grunge wannabes from California. But with the release of their second album—and every album after that—STP proved it was the one '90s group able to handle nearly every style pioneered by the best hard rock bands of the previous two decades.

Creating a sound that has survived much longer than the band's brief history, DeLeo drew from Jimi Hendrix, Jimmy Page, and Joe Perry, marrying their sonic bravado with an extraordinary appreciation of melodic pop, cool jazz, funk, and even Queen-like glam and kitsch. In the process, DeLeo put together one of the most devastating catalogs of catchy hard rock tunes to emerge from the 1990s. And, as superficial as it seems, DeLeo's uncanny physical resemblance to guitarists like Perry and Page made him a perfect poster boy for the power of Les Pauls and high-volume amplification.

BIOGRAPHY

Dean DeLeo was born on August 23, 1961, in New Jersey. A huge fan of his sister's Hendrix records, he learned to play guitar as a teen, often singing at family gatherings. His parents listened to old jazz and show tunes, but his life changed when he heard Zeppelin's *Physical Graffiti*. Suddenly he knew he wanted to rock. At the same time, his younger brother Robert took an interest in the guitar, and the two found themselves writing songs together, influenced by bands like Zeppelin, the Beatles, the Who, Yes, the Rolling Stones, and Rush. Dean eventually formed a local cover band—playing hard and progressive rock—and Robert filled in on bass.

Robert moved to California to try his hand at music. There, he met vocalist Scott Weiland at a Black Flag show. The two found out they were seeing the same girl, and when she left town, they decided to form a band. They added Long Beach drummer Eric Kretz but had a tough time finding the right guitarist. Robert persuaded Dean to move from Jersey and join the band in San Diego, and in 1988 Stone Temple Pilots was born (although at first it played under other names, including Mighty Joe Young, as well as Shirley Temple's Pussy and other variations of the letters STP—the "specially treated petroleum" used in car engines).

They slogged it out in the bars of San Diego, playing a hybrid of hard rock and punk that to the untrained listener was, at the time, classifiable as grunge. So as one of the most prominent SoCal bands to sound even remotely like they were playing grunge, the group was scooped up by Atlantic in 1992. That same year, STP released its debut, *Core*. The first album, which invited comparisons to Pearl Jam and Alice in Chains—in large part due to Weiland's Eddie Vedder-esque baritone voice and stage theatrics—was only nominally a grunge affair. Despite the reworking of some obvious hard rock clichés, DeLeo rose above the material with monstrously punishing riffs in songs like "Sex Type Thing" and "Crackerman." But it was the Zeppelin-esque "Wicked Garden" that hinted at what the band was really capable of.

However, the band was slammed by the press as being nothing more than California copycats of the Seattle sound. But *Core* sold exceedingly well, and the band went on tour, establishing itself as a feverish yet polished live act that bore little resemblance to the free-for-all antics of most grunge bands.

When STP's second album, *Purple*, arrived in 1994 it might as well have been an entirely different band. Gone were Weiland's lower-register moanings and the dark dungeon production values. Instead, the group emerged as a truly creative hard rock band, one that knew how to speed it up and slow it down, sometimes in midverse. Like Soundgarden, there were elements of pop, metal, and psychedelia in the music, but STP went to the further edges of rock, dabbling in just about everything they could find. There were touches of Bowie-era glam, British acoustic-Celt, Hendrixian acid rock, and even a nod to prog-rock orchestration and Burt Bacharach. All of it was tucked into a polished hard rock shell, best illustrated by the deceptively simple riffs to "Vasoline" and "Unglued." DeLeo's churning guitar and Weiland's vocal histrionics were the band's centerpiece (much like that of Cantrell and Staley in Alice in Chains), and together their sound was perfectly suited for arena-style hard rock. It was music made for flash-pots.

The cracks started to show the following year when Weiland was busted for heroin possession. This was the first of a long series of trips to court and the big house, turning Weiland into a habitual offender whose every roll of the dice landed him on the "go directly to jail" spot on the Monopoly board.

Once Weiland was out of rehab, the band returned with 1996's stunning *Tiny Music . . . Songs from the Vatican Gift Shop*, perhaps the single most musically diverse rock album released in the 1990s. With tunes like "Pop's Love Suicide" and "Trippin' on a Hole in a Paper Heart," the DeLeo brothers and Kretz proved to be the most interesting rhythm section in all of rock, while Weiland's vocals had taken on far greater range and dynamism than those of the people he had earlier been accused of imitating. Most notable was DeLeo's ability to create machine-grinding riffs with a pop sensibility, which resulted in a strange—and strangely accessible—sound that was equally at home on rock radio and on alternative stations.

CHECKLIST ✓

Guitar	Gibson Les Paul Standard		**Attack**	Varied, but usually in constant motion; not shy about right-hand noise
Setup	Standard			
Strings	.009–.046		**Signature traits**	Catchy and constantly cycling riffs, heavy tone
Pickups	Stock			
Amplification . . .	Primarily Demeter, VHT, Vox ACs		**Influences**	Jimi Hendrix, Jimmy Page, Steve Howe, Pete Townshend
Effects	Dunlop Crybaby wah, Boss Chorus pedal		**Overall approach**	Heavy, but hummable
Tone	Thick and bludgeoning			

SELECTED DISCOGRAPHY

Core (Atlantic, 1992)
Purple (Atlantic, 1994)
Tiny Music . . . Songs from the Vatican Gift Shop (Atlantic, 1996)
Talk Show (Atlantic, 1997)
No. 4 (Atlantic, 1999)
Shangri-La Dee Da (Atlantic, 2001)

RECOMMENDED CUTS

"Sex Type Thing" (*Core*)
"Crackerman" (*Core*)
"Vasoline" (*Purple*)
"Silvergun Superman" (*Purple*)
"Unglued" (*Purple*)
"Big Empty" (*Purple*)
"Pop's Love Suicide" (*Tiny Music . . .*)
"Trippin' on a Hole in a Paper Heart" (*Tiny Music . . .*)
"Down" (*No. 4*)
"Sex and Violence" (*No. 4*)
"Dumb Love" (*Shangri-La Dee Da*)
"All in the Suit That You Wear" (*Thank You*, Atlantic, 2003)

However, Weiland's habit of both ingesting heroin and landing on the wrong Monopoly square got in the way of the ensuing tour, so the band had to abandon what should have been its greatest commercial success (comparisons to Layne Staley were inevitable). Weiland drifted in and out of the group, taking time out from his usual stop at the county jail to record a solo record. The DeLeos got tired of waiting around and formed a one-off project with Kretz called Talk Show. The resulting album was stillborn, although notable for its continuation of the STP sound.

Surprisingly, Weiland and STP got together long enough to record *No. 4* in 1999, a seriously heavy effort that featured aggressive tracks like "Down," "Sex and Violence," and "Sour Girl." This album was as much a hard rocker as anything the band had ever done, and just as STP was ready to start touring . . . (we know this sounds like a broken record) Weiland was invited back to spend some time in a guarded correctional facility, courtesy of the state of California.

But the DeLeos and Kretz hung in there, picking Weiland out of the gutter one more time to put together 2001's *Shangri-La Dee Da*. Picking up where *No. 4* left off, DeLeo unleashed his now well-honed and laser-focused riffs on tunes like "Dumb Love" and "Coma."

And that was it. Weiland and the band couldn't do it any more. The DeLeos and Kretz packed it in, while Weiland joined the recovering addicts of Guns N' Roses and formed Velvet Revolver. Releasing a greatest-hits record in 2003, the DeLeo brothers turned their attention to producing other bands (notably Alien Ant Farm). Dean had done some studio work for other musicians during his STP years, and it's likely he will pursue that path in conjunction with production.

STP and DeLeo got a bad rap right out of the gate, but the truly inventive way they put together influences from metal and pop to Broadway and psychedelia has avenged them over the years. In fact, their music sounds less dated than that of many of their grunge and pop contemporaries from the 1990s and early 2000s, and it holds up well on repeated listening. DeLeo was at his best forging big, nearly anthemic riffs in the style of '70s rock bands, but he and the rest of STP threw in just enough musical curves to heighten the intensity level of everything they put out.

GEAR & SETUP

Dean DeLeo's gear choice is, at first blush, simple. He uses Les Paul Standards (usually '78s) played through a Demeter TGP-3 three-channel preamp and a VHT Classic stereo tube power amp. Getting the STP sound would be easy if it stopped there, but DeLeo's real gear selection is more like the back room at a vintage guitar supercenter. Here's a list that barely scratches the surface: Fender '67 Telecaster, Gibson Les Paul Special (with P90 pickups), Paul Reed Smith hollowbody, Danelectro electric sitar, Gibson ES-295, a Gretsch with a built-in speaker, a Guild Thunderbird—the list goes on, with more than 100 guitars in total, many from the 1960s. He brings a huge chunk of them into the studio and out on the road. He uses .010–.046 strings, although he will up them to .011s or .012s depending on the guitar.

Amps are also of the overflowing-warehouse variety. While relying primarily on the Demeter preamp and VHT Classic stereo tube power amp, he also has the following: Vox AC10, AC15, and AC30; Sovtek MIG 50; Ampeg B15, late '60s Marshall combos; and an SIB Varidrive built by some of Dean's friends. He'll mix and match all of this at any given time in the studio, opting to record through several amps simultaneously so that he gets a different tone on each track but doesn't have to overdub. Then he mixes the track to achieve the sound he wants. Another point: He doesn't record guitars in stereo. If he wants to broaden a part, he'll record multiple mono takes and sync up the tracks individually.

DeLeo strips down his amp choice for the road, however. The basics for his live sound are a split signal through a Varidrive tube preamp into a Vox AC30, and a Demeter TGP-3 preamp and a Rocktron Intelliverb into a VHT Classic stereo amp. These go into Marshall 4x12 cabinets. The setup goes into four microphones and is then mixed to create a layered sound that gives the effect of two separate players.

Effects are present, but only sporadically as DeLeo likes the tones from his guitar/amp combinations. The most obvious pedals are a Dunlop Crybaby wah and a Boss CE-1 chorus.

DeLeo uses several alternate tunings, including dropped D, DADFAD ("Lounge Fly"), and various open tunings for slide work.

STYLE & TECHNIQUE

Because DeLeo veers in and out of so many styles, he varies his technique from song to song. But when it comes to playing straight-ahead hard rock, he's pretty much balls to the wall. The riffs are fast and hard, with a jagged, dark metal tone that puts them out in front of everything but the vocals—and even that's an occasional competition. The riffs are meant to roll over and over, like a continuous cycle, and he rarely lets up on the onslaught. Like Dave Navarro, he fills up nearly every crevice of space available to the guitar, yet he does it with a restraint more in line with Jerry Cantrell's playing. Think of it as lots of controlled and tasteful layers built up to create one big sound (Navarro employs layers that often feature different parts, while Cantrell creates big sounds with plenty of air around them).

There is a heavy dose of Zeppelin in DeLeo's riffs, which lean more toward the experimental riffs found on *Physical Graffiti* than the more blues-oriented riffs on *Zeppelin I* and *II*. The same is true of DeLeo's solos, although they owe as much to Hendrix as they do to Page.

Like other hard rock players, DeLeo is at his best when he has the full backing of a tight rhythm section, and his brother and Eric Kretz provide exactly that. This gives him room to move around during his solo sections (like Page and Eddie Van Halen) without having to worry about the guitar carrying the rhythm weight at the same time.

Most important, DeLeo writes singable riffs and solos over uncommonly sophisticated chord changes. This comes from his appreciation of pop music. He cites Glen Campbell and Burt Bacharach as influences, and although modern listeners may scoff at the retro-lounge nature of these musicians, they both had keen ears for harmony and catchy hooks. DeLeo is capable of the same; his hooks are big, loud, and harsh, but they are as catchy as anything else you would hear on any type of radio station anywhere. DeLeo's guitar playing and songwriting are perfect examples of listening to everything you can and distilling the absolute best from it.

LESSON

Dean overdubbed a *lot* to get a super-thick wall of guitars, but many of his riffs would have come across powerfully on a lone ukulele. In our recording of **Ex. 1**, there's just one overdub. We used the same Les Paul, in fact—on the bridge pickup for the first take and on the neck pickup for the second.

For some rock 'n' roll snarl, get a little bend on the 6th-string notes. To recreate the cool choked harmonics in the verse riff, just lay the weight of your fingers directly over the fretwire on frets 5, then 4, then 3, then 2. With enough volume and drive, you'll be surprised how many places you can pick up harmonics; so much so, in fact, that you have to be careful to get your fingers *off* of any harmonics when you just want the choked strings, as in bars 6 and 10.

Track 25

Ex. 1

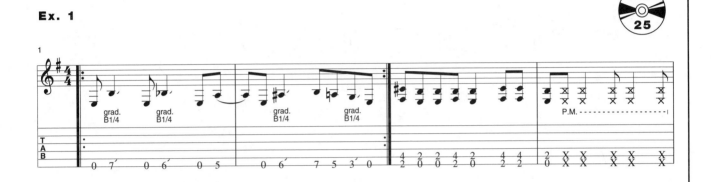

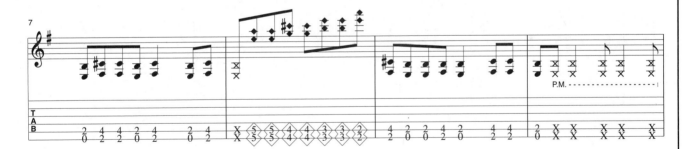

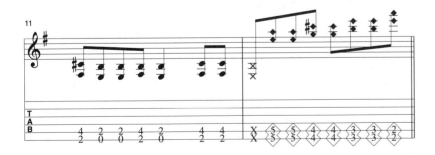

In **Ex. 2**, Guitar 1 plays a steady rhythm pattern while the bass line descends chromatically from *G* to *F♯*. But it's the next chord, *E♭maj7/B♭*, that really differentiates the progression. You'll need to back off your guitar's volume and limit amp gain to hear the notes of the chord. In bar 7, Guitar 2 enters with a sitar-like part with the droning open *G* string and the opening bend. A little vibrato when you come down from that bend (the 2nd-string, 7th-fret *F♯*) sweetens it up. To emulate DeLeo's tone, Guitar 2 was recorded through two separate amps, with one slightly overdriven.

Ex. 2

Track 26

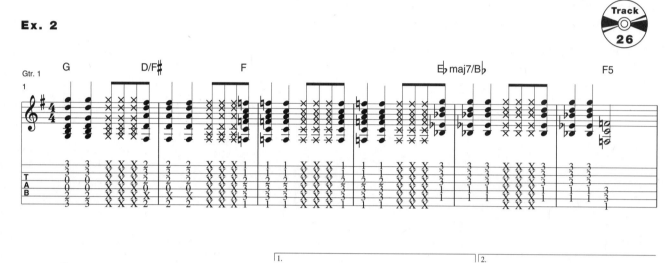

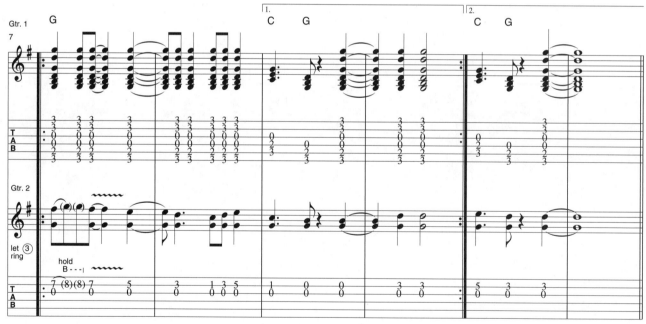

And now for something completely different. Dean and Co. pared their arrangements *way* down for a handful of times—both for intros to tunes like "Big Empty" and "Interstate Love Song" and for entire songs including "So I Know," "Pretty Penny," and "Daisy." Often a slide was heard over lounge-jazz changes, as in **Ex. 3**. Plunk out the progression in strict time on a bassy electric or even an acoustic. While the slide attacks should be clean and well muted—using fingers rather than a pick will help—your tone will benefit from slightly overdriving a low-wattage amp.

Ex. 3

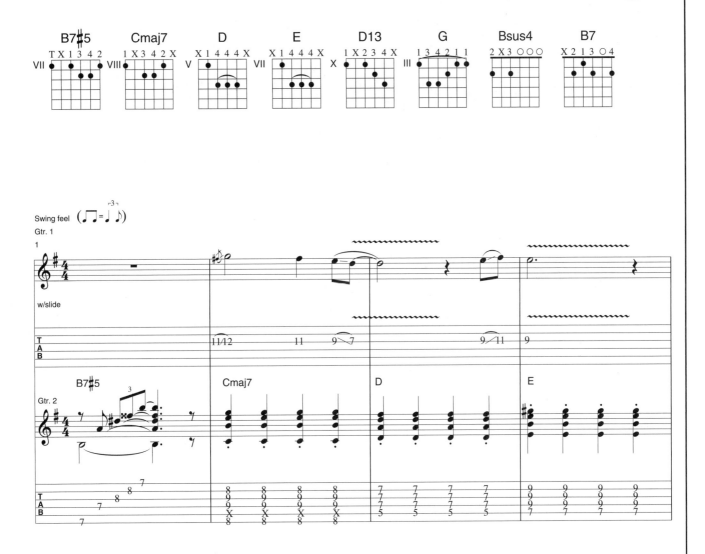

example continued on next page

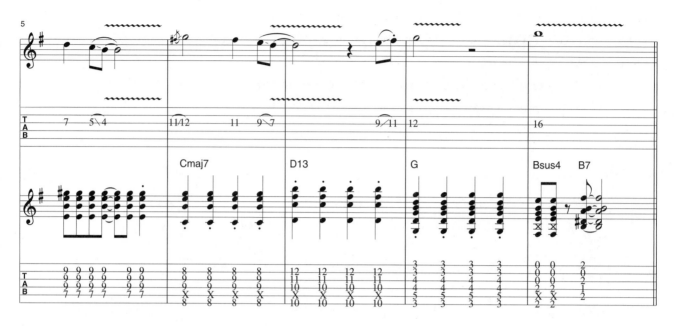

CHAPTER 8
Dave Grohl of Foo Fighters

If there's any justice in the world, Dave Grohl will be remembered as the frontman and guitarist for the Foo Fighters—and not the drummer for Nirvana. Even though Grohl may be one of rock's most accomplished drummers, the guitar, vocal, and songwriting chops he shows in the Foo Fighters make him one of the best all-around musicians of the millennium.

There are few guitarists anywhere who combine all the talents Grohl does. His ability to write big arena-style riffs and lighter, more intricate parts—coupled with an appreciation for maximum distortion—make him a much more impressive guitarist than most of the hard rockers working today. And there are precious few guitarists who are as good behind a microphone or drum kit as Grohl is behind the guitar. In the history of hard rock, he's in an elite class as a triple threat, setting the hard rock standard for this century.

BIOGRAPHY

David Eric Grohl was born on January 14, 1969, in Warren, Ohio, and grew up in Springfield, Virginia, a suburb of Washington, D.C. He picked up the guitar at age ten, influenced primarily by Led Zeppelin and Jimmy Page (later on he would mention his appreciation for Stevie Ray Vaughan and Warren Haynes of the Allmans and Gov't Mule). Grohl took lessons for a year but got bored because he wasn't learning the things he wanted to. Instead, he taught himself by ear, learning from Beatles and Zeppelin records. His first "real" guitar, given to him on his 12th birthday, was a Sears Silvertone with the amp built into the case. In addition to his interest in guitar, he was teaching himself drums in a rather unconventional fashion—by hammering a makeshift drum set made of pillows and chairs with marching-band drumsticks. His drumming influence was Zeppelin's John Bonham—he emulated Bonzo's playing by hitting everything as hard as he could.

Grohl transitioned from hard rock to punk when he started rummaging through his cousin's collection of hardcore punk records. He immersed himself in bands like Bad Brains and Minor Threat, adopting their frenetic styles for both his guitar playing and drumming. In his mid teens, he played guitar in D.C.-area cover bands before joining punk band Freak Baby as the band's guitarist. The band eventually kicked out its bassist, whose role was taken over by the drummer, so Grohl moved to the drums.

He was soon asked by local punk icons Scream to play drums, so he quit high school and joined them on the road. His bombastic and skilled approach to drums was notably better than the simple thrash and trash of most punk drummers, and he gained notoriety in punk circles as a drummer worth listening to. When Scream disbanded, he was recommended to Kurt Cobain after Nirvana fired drummer Chad Channing. Moving to Seattle in 1990, Grohl rounded out Nirvana's raw sound by adding dense rhythms that filled in the band's stripped-down proto-grunge style.

With Grohl in the drum seat, Nirvana's reputation as a live act grew substantially. The band signed to Geffen and in 1991 released *Nevermind*, an album that single-handedly changed the music industry in the '90s. With Cobain out front and Krist Novoselic on bass, Grohl left his guitar playing at home and stayed behind the drums, although he wrote—and sang lead—on songs that never made it to the band's records. After *Nevermind*'s release, though, Grohl took the opportunity to produce an indie cassette called *Pocketwatch* (the tune "Marigold" from this set later became a Nirvana B-side). While his primary gig was obviously as Nirvana's drummer, Grohl recorded his own songs and made demo tapes during the band's frequent recording and touring breaks.

When Cobain decided to join the heavenly chorus in 1994, Grohl found himself without a band. He gave serious thought to quitting the music business entirely (he didn't want to be known as "that guy from Kurt Cobain's band") until he dug up his demos and decided to record the best songs in a professional studio. After recording the vast majority of parts himself, he gave the finished tapes to friends. Unbeknownst to Grohl, word spread quickly about his catchy tape of hard rock songs recorded with a punk fury. Record companies came knocking at his door.

Signing with Capitol, he released the album as *Foo Fighters*. From the driving riffs and droning guitars of "I'll Stick Around" and "Good Grief" to the near-metal sludge of "Weenie Beenie" it was clear that Grohl could breathe life into a form that was clichéd and near death in the mid-1990s. The record proved to be an immediate success, so he enlisted former Nirvana stage guitarist Pat Smear and Sunny Day Real Estate's bassist Nate Mendel and drummer William Goldsmith, and took this full-fledged band out on tour.

CHECKLIST ✓

Guitars . . . . Primarily Gibsons: SG, Les Pauls, Trini Lopez, RD Artist; live, primarily Dan Armstrongs

Setup . . . . Standard

Strings . . . . Dean Markley

Pickups . . . . Stock, usually uses the treble pickup

Amplification . . . Vox AC30, Mesa/Boogie Rectifiers, Marshall JCM900

Settings . . . . Volume on full, slightly higher on treble than on bass, both up between 5 and 10

Effects . . . . ProCo Rat fuzzbox, Q-Tron envelope filter, Boss DD-3 digital delay, Electro-Harmonix Memory Man echo, Heil Talk Box, all used sparingly

Tone . . . . Big, fat, and warm

Attack . . . . Heavy, often fast and frenetic but under control

Signature traits . . . . Constant chord and riff movement, country influence on clean parts

Influences . . . . . . Jimmy Page, Bad Brain's Dr. Know

Overall approach . . . . Bombastic yet melodic and tasteful, all with a punk frenzy

SELECTED DISCOGRAPHY

Foo Fighters (Capitol, 1995)
The Colour and the Shape
  (Capitol, 1997)
There Is Nothing Left to Lose
  (RCA, 1999)
One by One (RCA, 2002)

RECOMMENDED CUTS

"I'll Stick Around" (*Foo Fighters*)
"Weenie Beenie" (*Foo Fighters*)
"Good Grief" (*Foo Fighters*)
"My Poor Brain" (*The Colour and the
  Shape*)
"Wind Up" (*The Colour and the Shape*)
"My Hero" (*The Colour and the Shape*)
"Everlong" (*The Colour and the Shape*)
"Stacked Actors" (*There Is Nothing Left
  to Lose*)
"Learn to Fly" (*There Is Nothing Left to
  Lose*)
"Aurora" (*There Is Nothing Left to Lose*)
"All My Life" (*One by One*)
"Times Like These" (*One by One*)

The success of the first record led to plans for a second, which was to be a full band effort. However, Goldsmith left, and Grohl recorded the drum parts himself before bringing in Taylor Hawkins. The result was 1997's *The Colour and the Shape*, which established Grohl and his band as much more than a post-Nirvana novelty, generating four singles in the process. Smear left after the record was released, replaced briefly by Franz Stahl, Grohl's former Scream band mate. That arrangement lasted only until the recording of 1999's *There Is Nothing Left to Lose*, when Stahl exited. After auditioning 35 guitarists, Grohl chose Chris Shiflett, who has hung onto the job ever since.

Despite the Spinal Tap–style lineup changes, Taylor Hawkins's near-fatal overdose, and Grohl's numerous side projects, the band returned with the stunning *One by One* in 2002. The record, which featured Queen guitarist Brian May, proved that Grohl could continue to push the boundaries of hard rock with a wider variety of styles and textures than the band had employed before.

Throughout their career, the Foo Fighters have been hailed as keeping hard rock interesting, not only with good songs, ferocious live shows, and incredibly entertaining videos, but also for Grohl's emergence as an exceptional frontman and guitarist. Grohl, however, has not limited himself to just the Foo Fighters. He played drums for the seriously heavy *Songs for the Deaf* release by Queens of the Stone Age, and then put out a heavy metal side project called *Probot*. That album featured a variety of guitarists, most notably Kim Thayil in a rare post-Soundgarden appearance.

Impressively, it has been Grohl's songwriting and thundering guitar that has made the Foo Fighters such an impressive band. Drawing on the abandon of punk combined with the stylistic experimentation of Led Zeppelin and the hooks of well-honed pop, Grohl has created a distinctive hard rock sound for the 2000s. His ability to play big-chord tunes with a unique riffing style has earned more recognition for him than Nirvana did, and his guitar playing proves that hard rock can take new and interesting forms in the right hands and fingers.

GEAR & SETUP

Grohl is a big fan of simple and loud. His guitars are the stock in trade of hard rock, mostly solidbody Gibsons: SG, RD Artist, Les Paul, and an Explorer. He also uses a semi-hollow Gibson Trini Lopez. Grohl is often seen onstage with an Ampeg Dan Armstrong (made of see-through Plexiglas), and he owns a Gretsch DuoJet and Fender Telecasters. His pickups are stock—whatever comes with the guitar. His strings are Dean Markleys with light-gauge tops and heavy bottoms.

His love of big, loud, and distorted sounds led him to the classic Vox AC30, the quintessential buzzbomb amp of the British invasion. He cites this as one of his primary amps because of its hot distortion. He also uses a Marshall JCM900, a Mesa/Boogie Dual Rectifier head going through Mesa/Boogie 4x12 cabinets, the Mesa/Boogie Maverick and Heartbreaker, and a Fender Twin.

In his search for pure distortion he keeps his signal chain fairly free of effects, although he does have a few in his arsenal: a ProCo Rat fuzzbox, a Q-Tron envelope filter, a Boss DD-3 digital delay, an Electro-Harmonix Memory Man echo, and a Heil Talk Box. Most of these are used for specific applications within a particular song; they are not layered on top of each other, nor are they used frequently. He occasionally uses a cigarette lighter as a slide.

In the studio, Grohl dials up a good amp sound and tends to stick with it throughout the recording process, though he's unscientific about creating and recreating those tones. He claims that with a good guitar/amp pairing—the RD through a Rectifier, the Trini Lopez through a Vox, the Tele through a Twin Reverb—he can get the sound he wants in ten minutes. The amps are cranked to 10 to get natural distortion, and away he goes. He has said he likes the sound of broken speakers or the sound of a speaker "getting its ass kicked." Settings are usually around 6 or 7 for treble and 8 for bass. The amps are typically miked in the studio as they are onstage, with a Shure SM57.

Grohl often records his guitars in one or two takes and then doubles them. (*The Colour and the Shape* was a notable exception: Wanting a cleaner, tighter sound, the band did as many as 30 takes for each track.)

Grohl seems to have a special soft spot for his Vox, even featuring one on a Foo T-shirt with the tongue-in-cheek slogan "Foo Fighters: Pop People with the Top Sound." He insists on including the amp in his backline onstage, even though his techs warn him that it always appears to be on the verge of breaking up and sounds like crap.

STYLE & TECHNIQUE

Grohl has said that he's never been a dexterous lead player, but his rhythm playing is beyond reproach. His style is percussive, as you'd expect from a drummer of his stature, but the real benefit of his drumming background is reflected in his ability to deliver a syncopated part with inflection and nuance—even when his volume is cranked to holy hell. His approach is one of constant movement—which pays homage to his history of punk playing—with a hard and thick edge that most punk lacked. But Grohl's guitars never slip into sludge 'n' grudge territory; on the contrary, some of his heaviest playing is offset by jangly, country-rock parts (many played on the Trini Lopez) that owe more to Gram Parsons than to Bad Brain's Dr. Know.

When Grohl is chording or riffing, he gives the impression of the guitar going nonstop, in a fluid, rolling fashion. Several Foo cuts include repeated riffs that cycle hypnotically, which not only gives them momentum but keeps attentive listeners pinned to the speaker as they try to figure out where exactly that downbeat is going to fall. He does have a penchant for employing staccato strumming when his chord changes are timed to cymbal crashes, "All My Life" and "Monkey Wrench" being prime examples.

Though many of his songs are, at their foundation, simple three-chord wonders, Grohl mixes up his playing so that it never sounds repetitive or formulaic. His sense of riffing is rooted in the best of pop, hard rock, and even metal, incorporating styles that are reminiscent of Tony Iommi and the Cult's Billy Duffy ("Live-In Skin," "Times Like These") and a right-hand technique that bests that of Metallica's James Hetfield. When not churning out riffs or perpetual-motion changes, Grohl allows his chords to ring out and sustain, letting his amp's overtones work to create a nice, thick sound. Like a lot of good hard rockers, he also has a deft touch on lighter tunes such as "Big Me," "Doll," and "Disenchanted Lullaby."

He occasionally employs alternate tunings, although they're quite simple. He has tuned his E string down to A ("Stacked Actors"), often uses dropped D ("Everlong," "Headwires"), and employed a modified dropped-D tuning with the B string tuned down to A ("MIA").

LESSON

Example 1 shows the type of intro on which Grohl might use his Trini Lopez on the bridge pickups through a Vox amp. He loves to open like this (similar intros are heard on "This Is a Call," "Big Me," "Ain't in the Life," "Next Year," "February Stars," and others), and he likes to butt a small intro part like this up against a big verse opener.

In most cases he'll offer up simple cowboy-chord strumming, revealing the clear thinking behind his songwriting. Note the differences, though. For one, the *G* chord doesn't get the root note on the bottom string till the end; instead, leave yourself freed up to catch the root as it begins a descending mid harmony on the 4th string.

Starting with a rinky-dink little tone like this can really make the song explode by contrast when it begins in earnest.

Ex. 1

Track 28

Grohl makes a lot out of a little, and the initial strumming in **Ex. 2** appears to be 99 percent attitude. But Grohl's guitar, overdriven though it may be, is building a rhythm bed (as you'll see in the next example). Hint from the "harder than you thought" category: Keep those eighth-note power chords in bars 5 through 8 robotically even—notice that there are no accented notes—and keep the palm muting really tight.

Ex. 2

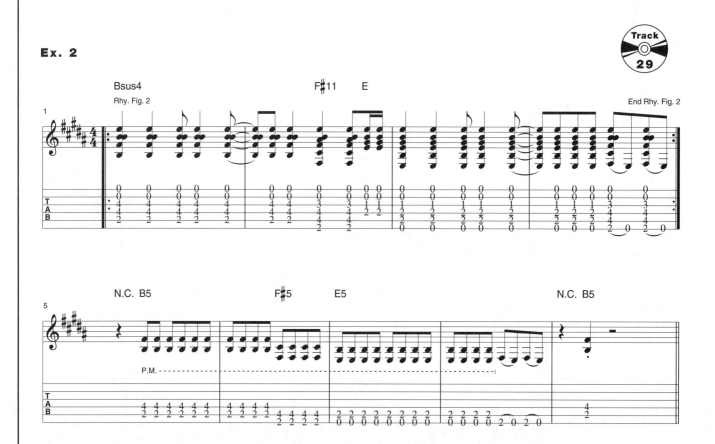

Sometimes one overdriven guitar just ain't enough, so we're going to add **Ex. 3**'s part to Ex. 2's. Like something out of Hüsker Dü, an assault of downstrokes is heard with open strings ringing. All movement in the first eight bars is on the 3rd string, and you'll have to move pretty quickly to catch every note.

The commotion comes to an abrupt stop with the steady low eighths, and a new round of tension builds. The guitar in the previous example played power chords at this spot (bar 5), but the single note here helps make for a tight sound and more space between notes.

Ex. 3

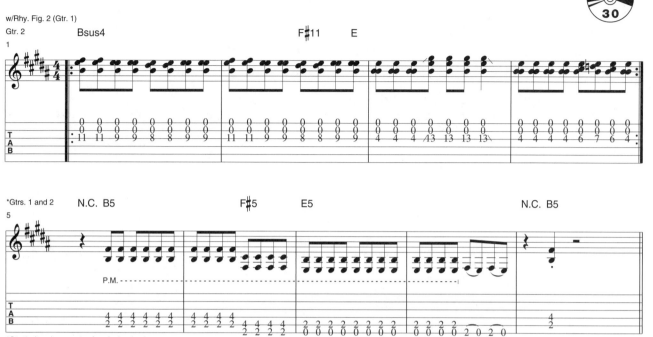

*Gtr. 2 plays lower note of each chord only.

Grohl gets hypnotic with many of his riffs and patterns, often the result of planting small figures that repeat but fall on a different beats in a four-bar cycle. He's done it both with heavy riffs ("Live-In Skin") and in more melancholy tunes ("Aurora," "Everlong").

When fingering the 5th-string notes in **Ex. 4**, let some of the meat of your left hand mute the low *D* so it doesn't ring over them. It's tempting to use pull-offs for this example in dropped *D*, but articulate every note.

This example mimics one of Dave's recording techniques. Two guitars play identical parts: One has a crisp overdrive (panned to about 10:30), like the type you might get from a ProCo Rat pedal, while the other one (2:30) has a natural tube sound overdriven till it sounds awful. You can hear the distortion tail on the right.

Ex. 4

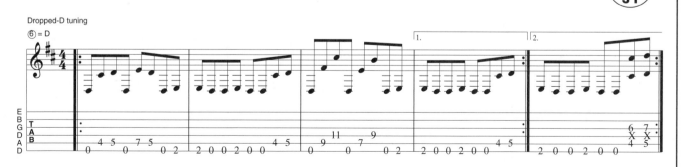

Here's another of the many ways Grohl lays down a hook (**Ex. 5**). Again, it's simple in nature, but nuance make all the difference.

For instance, catch the voices in the chords. The first time on the *B* chord, it's a suspended 4th—which masks whether the chord is major or minor—while the second time around reveals a *B* minor chord (bar 7). Rather than sit on it, though, the following measure opens up to *Bm7*.

A big fat melody is delivered over the changes, played entirely in octaves. A climb on the octaves over the *A* chord at the end begs the vocal line to come around and start the verse.

Ex. 5

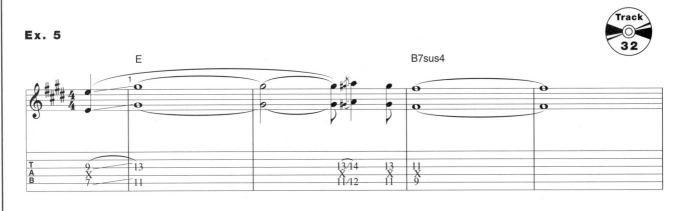

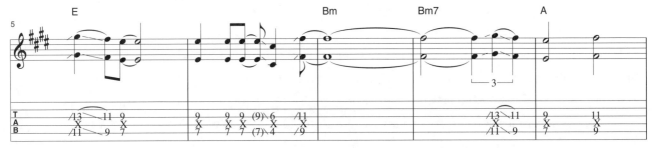

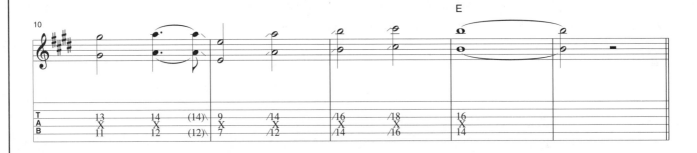

ON THE CD

Track 1: Ace Frehley Ex. 1

Track 2: Ace Frehley Ex. 2

Track 3: Ace Frehley Ex. 3

Track 4: Ace Frehley Ex. 4

Track 5: Angus Young Ex. 1

Track 6: Angus Young Ex. 2

Track 7: Angus Young Ex. 3

Track 8: Eddie Van Halen Ex. 1

Track 9: Eddie Van Halen Ex. 2

Track 10: Eddie Van Halen Ex. 3

Track 11: Eddie Van Halen Ex. 4

Track 12: Dave Navarro Ex. 1

Track 13: Dave Navarro Ex. 2

Track 14: Dave Navarro Ex. 3

Track 15: Dave Navarro Ex. 4

Track 16: Dave Navarro Ex. 5

Track 17: Kim Thayil Ex. 1

Track 18: Kim Thayil Ex. 2

Track 19: Kim Thayil Ex. 3

Track 20: Kim Thayil Ex. 4

Track 21: Jerry Cantrell Ex. 1

Track 22: Jerry Cantrell Ex. 2

Track 23: Jerry Cantrell Ex. 3

Track 24: Jerry Cantrell Ex. 4

Track 25: Dean DeLeo Ex. 1

Track 26: Dean DeLeo Ex. 2

Track 27: Dean DeLeo Ex. 3

Track 28: Dave Grohl Ex. 1

Track 29: Dave Grohl Ex. 2

Track 30: Dave Grohl Ex. 3

Track 31: Dave Grohl Ex. 4

Track 32: Dave Grohl Ex. 5

Track 33: Tuning

All tracks performed by Rich Maloof and recorded at OopStudios in Brooklyn, New York.

ACKNOWLEDGMENTS

The authors wish to acknowledge the following for their help in creating this book:

Thanks to our editors at Backbeat Books, Richard Johnston, Nancy Tabor, and Amy Miller—along with Publisher Matt Kelsey, sales manager Kevin Becketti, and publicist Nina Lesowitz—for giving us the opportunity to develop The Way They Play into a full-fledged series. This book follows *Blues Rock Masters*, *Acoustic Rock Masters*, and *New Metal Masters*—and there are more masters yet to come. Much appreciation to Jesse Gress for transcribing the music examples. Our thanks as always extends to Philip Chapnick, who encouraged us to find a home for The Way They Play within his publishing group.

Continued thanks to Bill Cummiskey of Fender Musical Instruments, and Paul Muniz at DigiTech/Harman Music Company.

Thanks yet again to Pete Prown, America's reigning guitar gear authority and professional contrarian. His acerbic commentary, poignant wit, and early curfew have made sure that we raise the bar every time we delve into another book. Pete's own books, *Gear Secrets of the Guitar Legends* (Backbeat Books) and *Legends of Rock Guitar* (Hal Leonard), are must-reads for any guitarist. Go out and buy them. Now.

HP Newquist would like to thank:

Thanks first and foremost to Rich Maloof, who made the words and ideas on these pages come to life via his spot-on guitar playing and editing. As a man of many talents, Rich is not to be underestimated, especially in the dead of night or when opening a bottle of Scotch. His friendship, attention to detail, withering cultural commentary, and scathing e-mails are of inestimable value.

Thanks to Trini, Madeline, and Katherine, the women who make it all worthwhile. They are the loves of my life for many reasons, not the least of which is that they have embraced the concept of electric and acoustic guitars as home furnishings.

Finally, thanks to those individuals who indirectly played a part in the creation of this book. To the members of the Pangborn Reunion '04, this is what I was doing while you were all off on the Notre Dame links. To the VideoWest engineers, who were amazed that Rich and I did this for a living. To John Kunkel, Thomas Werge, Tucker Greco and family, Michael S. Johnson and family, Lou Dobbs, and Al Mowrer. To my brothers, sisters, and parents for being as supportive and indulgent as any musician in a big family has a right to expect. To everyone else who taught me how to write a better sentence or figure out a difficult riff. Thanks, one and all.

Rich Maloof would like to thank:

My thanks to Harvey Newquist, who somehow managed to compose the bulk of this book while writing two others, teaching how neurons fire in the cerebellum, and seeking alternative energy sources in the Alexander Archipelago. The value of a generous and sophisticated friend who can also argue the merits of the "Sweet Leaf" riff should never go unappreciated.

It may give my orchestration professor a coronary to know this, but my love of music jelled when hard rock smacked me upside the head as a 12-year-old. Thank you, Ace Frehley.

For embracing, or at least tolerating, the kind of childishness exhibited herein, thanks and love to Kris. And for my second childhood, thanks to Daniel.

PHOTO CREDITS

ABOUT THE AUTHORS

HP Newquist and his writing have appeared in publications as diverse as *The New York Times, Rolling Stone, USA Today, Variety, Billboard,* and *Newsweek.* He has written a dozen books, including *Music & Technology* (Billboard Books), *The Great Brain Book* (Scholastic), *The Yahoo! Ultimate Reference Guide to the Web* (HarperCollins), *The Brain Makers* (Macmillan), and *Legends of Rock Guitar* (with Pete Prown, published by Hal Leonard). His magazine articles have covered topics from musicians, machines, and medicine on to artificial intelligence and virtual reality. His film credits include writing the Emmy-nominated music documentary *Going Home* for The Disney Channel.

Newquist is also the former Editor-In-Chief of *Guitar* magazine. He still plays hard rock on his 20-year-old SG as loud as the neighbors can stand it. Sometimes louder.

Rich Maloof is an independent editor and writer based in Brooklyn, New York. He has written dozens of instructional pieces for musicians, including three previous volumes of The Way They Play (with HP Newquist, published by Backbeat Books) and *The Alternate Tuning Reference Guide* (Cherry Lane). In 2003 Maloof authored *Jim Marshall: The Father of Loud* (Backbeat Books) and founded *InTune,* a classroom magazine for music students.

Maloof served as editor-in-chief of *Guitar* magazine until 1998, when he launched his own business. Among his clients to date are Berklee Press, *Billboard,* CNN, TrueFire, and Yahoo! He has been playing guitar for over 25 years and wishes someone else would carry the gear already.

WHEN IT COMES TO GUITARS, WE WROTE THE BOOK.

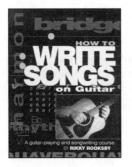